M000159301

INNERWILL

InnerWill

DEVELOPING BETTER PEOPLE, BRAVER LEADERS,
AND A WISER WORLD THROUGH
THE PRACTICE OF VALUES BASED LEADERSHIP

Dr. Thomas Epperson

INNERWILL
M E D I A

INNERWILL

Developing Better People, Braver Leaders, and a Wiser World through the Practice of Values Based Leadership

ISBN   978-1-5445-2681-2 *Hardcover*

978-1-5445-2680-5 *Paperback*

978-1-5445-2682-9 *Ebook*

978-1-5445-2683-6 *Audiobook*

Contents

Introduction

This book is about Values Based Leadership (VBL). VBL is based on the idea that when we live, work, and lead in alignment with our core values, we perform better, we feel happier, and others trust us more. By acting on our own values, by modeling and setting an example, we help others do the same. The challenge is that many of us don't really know what we value, and we have trouble doing so consistently and with skill.

This book is for everyone. At InnerWill, we believe that leadership is a choice, not a title, whether you are in a formal leadership role or if you just want to be the best version of yourself. The intent of this book is to help anyone use the Five Practices of Values Based Leadership at work, at home, and in their communities. My goal with this book is to help you be more effective wherever you go by sharing tools, stories, and lessons that can help you realize your potential, discover your purpose, and have a positive impact on those around you.

This book is meant to be practical. It is grounded in research and real-world experiences, honed by real people doing real work on themselves over many years. This book has its roots in a fourth-generation family business, Luck Companies, and all of the leaders who have transformed the organization into one of the most highly engaged workplaces in the United States. The content is drawn from leaders, authors, and thinkers from a variety of industries, as well as clients and board members from our leadership institute. This book is not meant to be a textbook or a scientific document, although it draws inspiration from both.

The book is organized around the Five Practices of VBL. You will find examples, stories, quotes, and exercises that will help you follow your own journey of self-development. The book is meant to be easy to read and can be lighthearted at times, although the work of leaders is often serious and challenging. If you want to dig into the science behind the Five Practices of VBL, I have provided select resources in the Appendix so you can do a little light reading of the corresponding scientific literature and explore the work of some of our favorite thinkers and authors.

This book is not filled with easy answers, although the practices can be used by adults at any stage of their lives. In fact, these practices are hard. Like building any new skill, they take discipline, effort, and most of all, practice over time. As human beings, we are messy works in progress, and sometimes we fail. Yet, with time and effort, we can all be more effective if we can make a few more leadership choices that line up with the person we want to be and the impact we want to have. The Five Practices of VBL do work if you do the work.

This book would not exist if not for all of those people who have come before us, who have studied and sweated and strived to be the best they can be. This book has contributions from many people, all of whom I am incredibly grateful for. For all of those who have shared their time and wisdom with us, thank you.

Finally, this book is about you and your choices. On our team, our board, and in our parent company, we believe that leadership focused on the success of others will make things better in our workplaces, in our communities, and in our families. And that is our ultimate goal. Through the practice of VBL, we want to develop better people, braver leaders, and a wiser world.

Thank you for reading, and more importantly, thank you for the positive impact you will make on those around you.

Prologue

Imagine yourself—confident in the path you're on but open to the bends and curves ahead. Working each day to be a little bit better, under no illusion that you are perfect, but not paralyzed by anxiety that you have to be. Comfortable in your own skin and willing to grow.

Imagine others, extraordinary not because they are superhuman, but because they are not. Filled with the potential to be amazing.

Imagine a workplace where people are happy and engaged. Where they feel valued and committed to the organization's goals. Where they have the skills they need to do their jobs. Where they enjoy the work they do and the people they do it with.

Imagine a world where everyone takes a moment to think about the impact they could have and then acts on it. Where everyone makes a few more choices to help, to inspire, to connect. To lead others in creating stronger families, communities, and institutions. Who choose to work first on themselves and then to help others. Who stand up for what they value and when they get knocked down—and they will—who get back up. Who have found the just-right place between the courage to act and compassion for others.

This book is about leadership. But not leadership as a title, or for those who are more talented, smarter, and more creative than the rest of us. It is about leadership as a choice—a choice to have a few more better days than bad, to work on ourselves, to have a positive impact on others. To choose to act on what we value, even when the world is telling us to sit down, to be quiet, or to wait our turn. This book is about developing our inner will to be and do amazing things. Things that we desperately need in our workplaces, families, and communities.

And it all starts with a choice.

A STORY ABOUT HOW OUR
LEADERSHIP JOURNEY BEGINS

My journey started with feedback.

We were going through an 18-month development program, and the facilitator, Guy Clumpner, told me my leadership team was going to give me feedback, and my job was to only say "Thank you" and ask "What else?" I was looking forward to it—I knew I had to grow and I might get emotionally hijacked in the process.

The next morning, the team started giving me feedback. Guy wrote all the feedback on flip chart paper and taped it to the wall. Each time someone gave me feedback, I would say, "Thank you," and ask, "What else?" By lunchtime, we had filled up the walls with flip charts and feedback.

At first, I was really mad about it. I went to my dad, who was CEO at the time, and I complained. "They don't know me. They don't understand what it's like. They aren't perfect either." He looked at me and asked, "Have you heard this feedback before?" I told him I had. "I've been telling you the same things. Am I wrong too?"

After that, I went home, feeling a little more humble. Then I asked my kids, "What can I do to be a better dad?" My youngest, Margaret, told me, "Whenever you get home, you are either working or are on the tractor. I want you to throw sticks in the creek with me and watch them float downstream." That's the hardest thing to hear, that your kids don't feel like you are spending enough time with them.

I made a commitment then to work on myself. To listen to the feedback I've been given and try to get better each day, both at work and at home. When it's all said and done, it's my work as a dad I'm most proud of. When Margaret's grown, she won't remember the things we bought her, but she'll remember all the times I played with her in the creek.

—CHARLIE LUCK, BOARD MEMBER, INNERWILL AND CEO, LUCK COMPANIES

CHAPTER 1

===

Values

Why do values matter?

Our values influence our choices, emotions, behaviors, and relationships.

"Values are how I was raised."

"My mom taught me to be honest."

"I always follow my values."

"I'm a good person—I have values."

"I learned my values by doing the exact opposite of my family."

When you ask about values, most people share where their values come from or what they believe. We seem to instinctively grasp the idea that we are walking around with a set of beliefs that drive us, a set of beliefs about what is right and good. Since this book is all about leading with values, it is helpful to define what we mean by *values*.

For individuals, values guide our behaviors and decision making. Values consist of beliefs and assumptions about how the world works. Values can be obvious—like flashing signs on a dark night, pointing out the road ahead—or they can be subtle and just at the edge of our awareness, nudging us to make the right choice.

We all have values—obvious or not—and they move us to action. We develop our values over time and experiences, beginning when we're young. According to developmental psychologists, we begin to form assumptions about the world as we observe our parents, siblings, and relatives going about their days. Pretty soon, we're trying things we've seen modeled for us: which earns us rewards or punishments, which reinforce some assumptions and weaken others. We begin to develop a mental blueprint of how the world works. What started as assumptions become beliefs, and those beliefs coalesce into our values. Over time, our values become ingrained in us—literally wired into our brains—which makes them relatively enduring over the course of our lives.

ASSUMPTIONS **BELIEFS** **VALUES**

Values are tightly enmeshed with our emotions. Want to know what you value? Think back to the last time you experienced a strong emotion—happiness, sadness, anger, or joy. Chances are, if you pull back the covers, you'll find one of your values at the heart of the experience. Maybe you value honesty and someone lied to you. Maybe you value family and the kids came home to visit. Maybe you value respect and someone was rude. Maybe you value hard work and you spent the day getting a lot of things done. Whenever you experience a strong emotion, it involves one of your core values.

Given that our values are hardwired in us and have a direct line to our emotions, it's no wonder that they have such a strong influence on our behavior. For example, consider your career. Ever work for an organization that did not value what you value? How was the experience? Fulfilling? The best ever? Did you jump out of bed thinking, "I can't wait to go to work today!" More likely, you woke up thinking, "Please, not another day." You probably spent most of the time at work irritated or even angry, and certainly unhappy. Maybe you cut off a few people in traffic on the drive home, then yelled at the dog and kicked your houseplants. (Don't worry—that ivy had it coming.)

Consider your relationships. Specifically, that special person in your life who makes you crazy, who breathes the wrong way and sets you off. That person who always seems to grind on your nerves, even when you are working really hard to stay calm and be positive. It could be that he is a terrible person, or it could also be that he is a decent human being who happens to value different things than you. The conflict between the two of you is not about right and wrong but right versus right. You value independence; he values control. You value tasks; he values relationships. Eventually, these differing values lead to tension, sometimes to arguments, and perhaps to some dramatic showdowns or passive-aggressive avoidance.

Values have an upside as well, especially when we have jobs that are a close fit for our deeply held beliefs. Research shows us that in these periods of our lives, we perform at higher levels and feel more satisfied with our work. When we join organizations that value similar things to us, we feel more engaged and committed to the organization and its goals. We have more better days than bad.

That's not to say we should only seek out people with similar values and fill our workplaces with like-minded people. Building relationships with people who have different values than we do requires us to develop new ways of thinking, especially as we strive to be more effective. Working in organizations and on teams that are diverse can spark better ideas and more innovation, even as members cope with conflict sparked by those differences. These conditions may lead us to reflect on our assumptions and beliefs only to decide they no longer serve us well. And yet, working in jobs where we can be authentic or our true selves gives us the chance to be our best. Struggling every day to fit into a workplace that emotionally hijacks us for eight or more hours a day is not good for our mental well-being.

Given that some of our values are obvious and some are subtle, it often takes work to discover what we really believe. We feel like we "should" hold certain values because other people say so. Using language like "should" or "ought to" is a great indicator that values are not authentic to us. It's the voice of other people in our heads, scolding us about what they think we should be doing. It's the voice of guilt and anxiety, not the voice of our true selves.

Understanding our true selves takes time and energy, and we may discover things about our assumptions, beliefs, and values that we don't particularly care for. One of my teammates assumed she had to be funny to be a great teacher and has always believed that she was not funny. Since she values competence and wants to be good at whatever she undertakes, she had never tried teaching. Through coaching, reflection, and hard work on herself, she now understands that she does not have to be funny to be a great teacher. Moreover, she has found that she is actually very funny and has been a great addition to our team—as a teacher. For years, she walked around with an incorrect assumption and a limiting belief that held her back.

Our values may change over time as we go through different stages of life: single, married, divorced, with kids, without kids, employed, unemployed, retired. Many of our values are stable and enduring throughout our lives but may take on new meanings in new situations. For example, having kids did not change who I am as a person, but it certainly shaped and honed what I believe about the world and how I walk through it.

There are values we carry throughout life no matter the circumstances, but we may not realize they are with us. For example, I never considered that I valued family. Then I realized I spent all my time, money, and energy on my family. More importantly, I recognized that my family is my greatest sense of joy and satisfaction. Looking back, my value for family shaped my decisions from an early age. The older I get and the more I reflect on my behavior and my beliefs, the more I've come to realize that family, for me, is primarily about taking care of the people I'm close to, be it my kids or our friends or my team.

Our values are central to our effectiveness as leaders. In this book, we will explore a leadership philosophy based on values that can help us become better people, braver leaders, and contribute to a wiser world through something called Values Based Leadership.

Values-Based Leaders choose to live, work, and lead in alignment with their core values and ignite the potential of others by helping them do the same.

CHAPTER 2

Values Based Leadership

Values Based Leadership (VBL) means choosing to live, work, and lead in alignment with our core values and igniting the potential of others by helping them do the same. Let's take the definition further by exploring the ideas behind it.

LIVING, WORKING, AND LEADING IN ALIGNMENT WITH OUR CORE VALUES

A broad range of research from scientists such as Jim Kouzes, Milton Rokeach, and William Gardner has shown that when we act on our values, we feel less anxiety and more security. We perform better. We are more confident in our decisions. We are ultimately more effective in the eyes of others, especially when our words match our actions. When we walk our talk, others trust us, even if they disagree with us. We experience less conflict because others know what to expect from us and our behavior is consistent. More often than not, we are the best version of ourselves.

When we live, work, and lead in alignment with our core values, others see us doing so. In small and large ways, we serve as an example for how others can be authentic and how they can act on what is most important to them. Setting an example—or modeling—is a powerful teaching tool. Modeling is how we first developed as kids, by watching our parents. We continue to learn from models throughout our lives, seeing examples we want to follow and examples that turn our stomachs.

As formal leaders, we are always onstage, with an audience paying attention to our words and actions. When there is agreement, the audience is moved. When there is a break between who we say we are and what we do, the audience is at best annoyed and at worst distrustful. Sometimes the audience adopts our beliefs, and sometimes they don't. The lesson is not for the audience to value the same things we do but to discover what they value and learn that they can be their true selves. They can live, work, and lead in alignment with their core values. When they do, they will perform at a higher level and get better results. In some ways, this is enough to tap into the audience's potential, to help them discover and live into the best version of themselves. In other ways, the audience will also require support, feedback, challenges, and transparency about our own struggles.

Formal leaders are always onstage.

IGNITING THE POTENTIAL OF OTHERS

Potential is having the capacity to be or to do—we all have the potential to be the person we want to be, to accomplish the things we choose to accomplish. Reaching our potential means being able to realize more of our dreams, to break through our limitations and achieve more than we imagine.

That's not to say it's easy; reaching our potential takes work and effort. It's something we must seek out over and over again and strive to reach. Realizing our potential requires working on our skills and developing our abilities. The world does not always make it easy on us—life creates obstacles to growth. The people we surround ourselves with may limit us; they may not invest in our well-being, or they may try to make us feel smaller. If we feel that the obstacles are impossible to overcome, it will be difficult to become more than who we are today.

Life also creates opportunities for growth, which may masquerade as obstacles. Reaching our potential requires us to see the opportunity in challenges and to believe in our ability to learn from setbacks, which is no small feat. Reaching our potential is not a solo sport. We need others, and others need us.

When we ignite someone's potential, we increase their capacity to be and do. We help them overcome obstacles and seize opportunities to grow as they become the best version of themselves. By living, working, and leading in alignment with their own values, they are more likely to reach that potential and to realize more of their dreams.

LEADERSHIP AS A CHOICE

The goal of VBL is to have a positive impact on the lives of others—to ignite their potential. Having a positive impact on others starts with a choice to act on our values. We don't have to—think of all the people who say they value integrity but are not honest. Think of those who believe they value people but treat others as tools. Think of the times when we don't stand up for our values because we might be punished, lose a job or even a spouse. Those choices diminish us, and we get further and further away from our true selves.

It is also a choice to make a positive impact on others. Modeling is important, but it is not enough. We can choose to help others discover their true selves, to develop their skills and abilities, to grow and develop over time. Or we could choose to diminish them. To hold them back. To fail to give them the tough feedback they need to grow. To discourage them from looking inward or doing the hard work of being themselves all the time.

Above all, VBL is a choice. A choice to live, work, and lead in alignment with our core values. A choice to ignite the potential of others. A choice to make a positive impact.

Charlie Luck, CEO of Luck Companies, puts it this way: "My purpose in life is to help people reach their wildest dreams. Everyone has dreams and aspirations. But we all need other people to get there. If I can manage the eight-pound monster on my shoulders, choose to be more understanding and compassionate and a little less relentlessly driven, then I can focus on helping others figure out what they need to reach their dreams. But that means I have to work on myself first."

This choice is not always an easy one. We named our firm and this book *InnerWill* because of the inner will required to accept hard truths about yourself and your leadership. The inner will required to work on yourself, to constantly strive to be the best version of yourself. The inner will to make hard choices that align with your values but have a significant personal cost. The inner will to care so much about another person that you give them the hardest feedback they have ever had. The inner will to spend years becoming the person you want to be and create the impact you want to make.

Imagine if you could make a few more choices that line up with your deepest held beliefs. It would be impossible for us to perfectly act on our values—as Guy Clumpner, President of Holt Development Services, says, "We are human beings, not perfect beings." But imagine if you could make a few more choices to act on what you believe. Imagine if you could make a few more choices to ignite the potential of others. Think of what you could achieve.

Think of the impact.

The purpose of this book—and why our firm InnerWill exists—is to help individuals, organizations, and families have a greater positive impact on others through the practice of VBL. To help people live, work, and lead in alignment with their core values. To ignite the potential of others. The leadership required to have such an impact is significant—it takes work. It can be frustrating, and at times, you may feel like you are the only one trying. But take heart—this journey is amazing and fulfilling and can make a real difference in your life and your organization and even your family. And like any kind of change we want to make in our lives, the journey starts with work on ourselves first.

VBL for individuals includes Five Practices that, if used again and again over time, will help you become a better leader. In my case, they also helped me become a better father and husband, and overall a better human being. Not to say that I was terrible before taking my first step on this journey, but I was no picnic. Just ask my brothers.

The book is organized by each of the Five Practices, starting with an overview, then exploring each of the practices and supporting behaviors in turn. Along the way, we will share real stories of leaders who have experienced VBL and been on their own journeys of self-development. We will provide exercises and resources you can use to help you along the way. Like any trip worth taking, it's not just the destination that matters; it's the journey itself. And that journey begins with a choice.

KEY TAKEAWAYS
- Values guide our behaviors and decision making.
- Values are made of our beliefs and assumptions.

- VBL means living, working, and leading in alignment with your core values and helping others do the same.

Understanding our values allows us to make choices that line up with who we want to be and the impact we want to make.

CHAPTER 3

The Five Practices of Values Based Leadership

Why do the Five Practices of Values Based Leadership matter?

The practices are the basic tools we need for our leadership journey.

When you consider leadership, do you think of a CEO, a politician, a school principal, the general manager of a team, or a pastor? Although these roles are important, the people in them are not necessarily leaders. A position does not make you a leader; your behavior does.

Consider this: your role, no matter what it is within an organization, a community, or even your family, is to lead, no matter what your title is or what your kids call you. We believe that leadership is a choice, not a title, and that leaders have the opportunity and responsibility to have a positive impact on other people. As a choice, Values Based Leadership occurs between people, and it always starts with you.

Leadership is a choice, not a title.

The process of Values Based Leadership includes Five Practices:

1. Building Awareness
2. Realizing Potential
3. Developing Relationships
4. Taking Action
5. Practicing Reflection

These practices are interdependent instead of linear; one does not lead to the other. These practices spin together like the gears of an engine. When all the gears are moving, the engine is performing well. When one of the gears is out of line, the engine loses power and may seize up.

BUILD AWARENESS

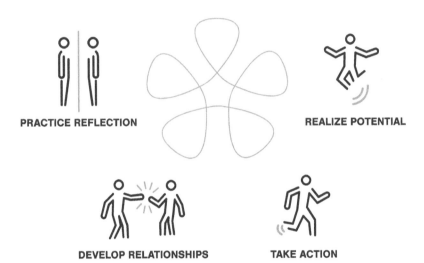

PRACTICE REFLECTION

REALIZE POTENTIAL

DEVELOP RELATIONSHIPS

TAKE ACTION

BUILDING AWARENESS OVERVIEW

The practice of Building Awareness is the process of understanding who we are. It includes:

- Examining our values, style, and beliefs
- Identifying our strengths and weaknesses
- Seeking out feedback

Building awareness can continue throughout our lives. As we evolve, take action, and develop relationships, our awareness changes. Awareness is a tricky thing; we may believe one thing about our strengths only to find out we were wrong. We may think we are impacting others one way but actually have a very different result than what we intended.

REALIZING POTENTIAL OVERVIEW

The practice of Realizing Potential means investing in our future. It includes:

- Discovering our purpose
- Developing our best self
- Pursuing ideal environments

Realizing Potential is the search for the best version of ourselves. It means exploring the big questions like why we are here and what we are meant to do. It requires us to define what impact we want to have on others. It means developing ourselves so we can live up to that purpose. It means finding the workplaces, communities, teams, or families that bring out the best in us, energize us, and make us better.

DEVELOPING RELATIONSHIPS OVERVIEW

The practice of Developing Relationships means building trust with others. It includes:

- Understanding others' values, styles, and beliefs
- Empathizing with others
- Supporting the success of others

Developing Relationships is ultimately about understanding what others think, feel, and need. It is a practice based on developing and strengthening our relationships by considering how others feel, even when we disagree. It means accepting others for who they are without needing to fix them, change them, or make them less than they are. It means looking for opportunities to help others be successful and, ultimately, building trust with them.

TAKING ACTION OVERVIEW

The practice of Taking Action means leading with courage. It includes:

- Making conscious choices
- Acting with our values
- Facing challenges

Taking Action is about making intentional choices that align with our deepest held beliefs. It means standing up for what we believe is right, especially when others tell us to stand down. Taking Action builds our ability to bounce back, to get back up when we get knocked down, to get back into the fray. It is a measure of our stick-to-it-ness, or grit, and our willingness to run toward the fire instead of away from it.

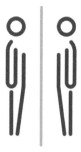

PRACTICING REFLECTION OVERVIEW

The practice of Practicing Reflection is about pausing to learn. It includes:

- Reviewing our thoughts, actions, and impact
- Learning from experience
- Applying the lessons

Practicing Reflection is about learning from our experiences. It is about gathering information on our values, our behaviors, and our impact on others and using that data to make decisions. It is about being mindful, developing awareness of what we are thinking, feeling, and experiencing in the moment in a nonjudgmental way. Ultimately, Practicing Reflection is about applying what we have learned to become the best version of ourselves over time, to live into our purpose and realize our potential. We reflect so we can make choices that better align with who we are and the person we want to become.

These Five Practices of Values Based Leadership have a cumulative effect over time. By choosing to act on them again and again, we develop our skills and increase our effectiveness. We become more authentic and influential. We become who we are meant to become and do what we are meant to do. We are better able to live for our purpose, on purpose.

In the next few sections, we will discuss each of the Five Practices and share practical tips on how to act on them. We will offer exercises to prompt your thinking and inspire you to take action. We will work on being better people, braver leaders, and a wiser world through the practice of Values Based Leadership.

KEY TAKEAWAYS

There are Five Practices of Values Based Leadership:

1. Building Awareness
2. Realizing Potential
3. Developing Relationships
4. Taking Action
5. Practicing Reflection

Using these Five Practices will help us grow as leaders and make a positive difference in the lives of others.

WHY "PRACTICES"

We see leadership as a choice, not a title—you don't have to be a formal leader to practice it, and you don't have to be at work to use it. We also see leadership as a process that happens *between* people, not *to* them. We focus on the practices of Values Based Leadership because they are choices you make again and again in the moment and over time.

A STORY ABOUT BUILDING AWARENESS

I was in my seventh year at Holt CAT. I was managing people but certainly not leading them. I'd grown up in a household with a single mother trying to raise four kids, but I had always been told I was special and thought pretty highly of myself. That year, Holt was in the midst of significant growing pains. Our owner, Peter Holt, decided that some things needed to change: one of those things was to learn about leadership. We went out to his ranch and had the first of many classes, which I expected to provide us with "weapons of mass instruction" to use on others. In that first class, I received an assessment that opened my eyes and created some significant emotional awareness. That assessment enlightened me about the strengths and limitations of having a *dominant and interactive* behavioral style. I was focused on results—at work and as a spouse and parent. With limited self-awareness, I was doing what I was emotionally and culturally wired to do, but it didn't make me effective. I realized I wasn't self-aware. When I got home, I shared with my wife that the class wasn't what I expected. Then I asked her for feedback about the assessment. In her charming way, she noted that I had little attention to detail, all the patience in the world (since I hadn't "used any" to date), and noted that active listening was not a behavioral strength. If feedback is a gift, that day was like Christmas! In retrospect, she gave me a lifetime pre-scription. And the "medicine" I still take over 30 years later was the catalyst to my success as a husband, parent, leader, teacher, and coach.

—GUY CLUMPNER, BOARD MEMBER, INNERWILL,
PRESIDENT, HOLT DEVELOPMENT SERVICES

CHAPTER 4

Building Awareness

Why does Building Awareness matter?

Whenever we decide to work on ourselves, to become more effective, we need a realistic understanding of who we are and the impact we have on others.

Imagine looking in a mirror.

What do you see? A son, a daughter, a wife, a husband, a mother, a father? A friend? Someone who is filled with potential, or someone who is flawed and struggling? A follower? A leader?

Do you see your strengths? What's easy for you, what you are good at doing, and what has made you successful? Or do you see your weaknesses? Those things that you struggle with or make you feel clumsy, foolish, or incompetent? Perhaps you see the negative results of overusing your strengths?

Do you see what's most important to you? What you believe and assume to be true? Do you see what you value?

Do you see the impact of all these things? On you and on others?

Early in my career, I thought of myself as a laid-back surfer dude. I thought I didn't let much get to me, that I was calm and patient, and that I took the waves as they came. I also thought I must be a real pleasure to work with because I was so easygoing.

When I started getting feedback and building my self-awareness, I came to find out that I am not laid-back. I am not calm or patient. I do not take the waves as they come; I charge through them. I was called intimidating, arrogant, uncaring, a workaholic, and intense. In short, I found out I'm not a surfer. I'm a shark.

I have thick skin. I'm not particularly curious about how other people feel. I'm incredibly task-focused, and like a shark, I'm afraid if I stop swimming, I'll drown. If you get between me and a job that needs to be done, I might eat you. And if you betray me or my team, you're gonna need a bigger boat.

We get formal and informal feedback throughout our lives, first from our family, then through school and friends, and eventually through work and everyday interactions with other people. Feedback is plentiful if you look for it. There are key themes I have heard for decades, but I am still surprised to hear something new. And I keep hearing new things.

It is not that I am closed-minded and naive about who I am. It's not that I'm worse than others, although I'm sure I still have blind spots you can drive a truck through. I think all in all, I'm average when it comes to my self-awareness. Some are more mindful about who they really are and the impact they have, and some are less so. In my experience, our awareness is generally quite low and only through sustained work, over time, do we begin to understand who we really are, which, while amazing and important, can feel like a root canal on the best of days.

Feedback is plentiful if you look for it.

Self-awareness is a key part of Values Based Leadership. How will we know what to do if we don't understand the impact of our choices? Yet, we are more complicated and deeper than we give ourselves credit for. The goal of Building Awareness is to understand who we are and the impact of our behaviors. To look in the mirror, to see ourselves as clearly as we can, including the good, the bad, and the ugly. To acknowledge that all of those things make us who we are but do not define us. We get to choose.

Joseph Luft and Harrington Ingham developed a building awareness tool in the 1950s they called the Johari window (based on their first names, Joe and Harry). The idea is that there are things we are aware of and that others are aware of. Everyone can see them clearly. There are also things about us that we are aware of but others are not. In this case, it's an opportunity for us to share and be transparent about what we are thinking and feeling. There are things about us that others can see clearly but we can't see at all—these things live in our blind spots. If we want to increase our awareness, gathering information about what others can see but we cannot is critical. And finally, there are things about us that we and others have not discovered yet. This is an opportunity for exploring and experiencing new things. By engaging with others through feedback and dialogue, we begin to close our blind spots while expanding what others understand about us. In turn, we begin to see the impact of our behaviors more clearly.

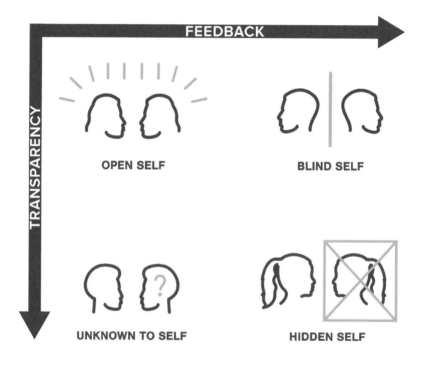

Building Awareness can be one of the most difficult parts of leadership. Feedback can feel threatening and hurtful. It can be surprising to learn how others experience us, especially when it does not line up with how we see ourselves. We might not like the person we see in the mirror, staring back at us. On the other hand, we may love the person we see and feel no reason to change.

Moreover, Building Awareness is difficult because we judge ourselves on our intent and what's going on inside our heads; others judge us on our behavior. We are incredibly good at justifying our actions while condemning the actions of other people. That can make it tricky for us to really hear, then accept feedback that contradicts our own ideas.

Another challenge is that we change over time and space. What may have been true about us at 20 years old is no longer true at 40 or 60. Our situation, relationships, and environments change, drawing on different parts of our gifts and gaps. In the 1930s, the psychologist Kurt Lewin described our behavior as an equation: $B = f(P,E)$. This equation is a fancy way of saying our behavior is a function of the person and the environment. Your behavior might change in different situations—like home instead of work, for example—which means you may get different feedback in different settings.

Building Awareness is an ongoing process. Like much in leadership, it is never one and done.

There are three ways we can practice Building Awareness:

1. Examining our values, style, and beliefs
2. Identifying our strengths and weaknesses
3. Seeking out feedback

EXAMINING OUR VALUES, STYLE, AND BELIEFS

Values, style, and beliefs define our personalities; they are that combination of psychology and brain structure that describes who we are and can, in certain situations, predict our behavior. One way to think about values, style, and beliefs is the metaphor of a house.

Our behavior is the exterior, the part of our house that everyone can see. That part of our personality is conscious to us.

Our personality style are the rooms of the house. The rooms may describe different parts of our personality, like the extroverted living room painted in bright colors or the introverted bedroom that is quiet and calm. Others infer what our personality style and preferences are based on our behavior—like judging the interior of a house by what the exterior looks like.

Our values are the floor of the house. Along with the beliefs and assumptions they are built on, they underpin our personalities. Sometimes our values are obvious, and sometimes they are subtle and indistinct, like hardwood hidden under carpet. Others can guess at our values, but even we don't know them for sure without lots of reflection. Sometimes you have to pull up the carpet to know for sure.

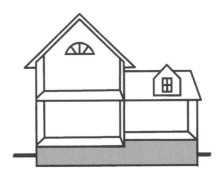

Finally, the foundation of our house is built on our beliefs and assumptions. We may not see how our house's foundation shapes our behaviors in ways that may be helpful or hurtful. They may have served us once, and we may have outgrown them. Or they may be based on faulty information. If the foundation of our house is rickety, the whole house will be impacted.

PERSONALITY STYLE

Humans have been studying personality since there have been humans. Ancient people focused on the natural world, such as air, earth, fire, and water, and attributed human behaviors to these elements. Others used animals—eagles, lions, deer, fish—to better categorize and understand behavior. The Greeks, then Romans and Islamist physicians focused on the four humors—blood, yellow bile, black bile, and phlegm—substances in the body they believed influenced a person's personality. (If someone in your life is an emotionless jerk, maybe they have too much phlegm!)

In the modern era, psychologists and scholars have developed a variety of assessments and tools to describe personality traits. Personality styles may include descriptors such as openness and curiosity, extroversion or introversion, confidence or nervousness, task focus or relationship focus, a preference for making decisions based on emotion or on logic and facts, or a preference for high structure versus low structure.

There are many personality tools, including the Five-Factor Model, Myers-Briggs, DiSC, and Insights Discovery, each with its own strengths and drawbacks. Academics have argued the merits of various tools and conducted research to validate the effectiveness of these assessments over time. In general, our behavior is a combination of our personality and situational factors; these instruments provide data for us to consider when Building Awareness, but they often fall short of explaining everything about a complex human being.

Many style assessments are based on psychologist Carl Jung's work on personality functions. In general, these models focus on an individual's preferences for extroversion or introversion (where you get your energy and where you focus), and thinking or feeling (how you prefer to make decisions, whether that is based on logic and facts or emotions and relationships).

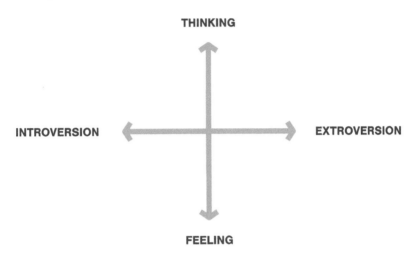

Some people have a preference for extroversion and for thinking; in general, this means they focus on tasks and make decisions based on facts, not people. They tend to be decisive and to the point, feel comfortable with conflict, and on bad days, they tend to ignore the emotional needs of others, trampling them as they try to get more stuff done.

Some people have a preference for extroversion and feeling; in general, this means they are relationship focused and make decisions based on how they and others feel. They tend to be sociable and talk to think. They have lots of casual relationships, love to be entertained, and have FOMO, fear of missing out. On bad days, they may come across as dramatic or unfocused.

Some people have a preference for introversion and thinking;

in general, this means they focus on accuracy and logic. They tend to be quiet observers who love to collect more information on issues. They are curious and precise. On bad days, they may appear to others as cold and impersonal, and they may overly criticize ideas not out of malice but because they want to help by pointing out the flaws. They may also have JOMO, the joy of missing out.

Some people have a preference for introversion and feeling; in general, they focus on feelings and one-on-one relationships. They tend to prefer harmony and want everyone to quietly get along. They tend to be good listeners and observers, although they may be run over by people with more extroverted and direct personalities. They may internalize bad feelings until they build up a deep and unbending grudge that they keep on the inside unless cornered.

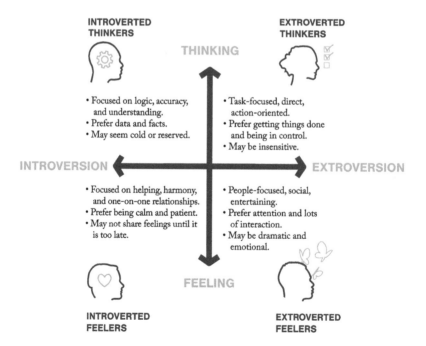

INTROVERTED THINKERS

- Focused on logic, accuracy, and understanding.
- Prefer data and facts.
- May seem cold or reserved.

EXTROVERTED THINKERS

- Task-focused, direct, action-oriented.
- Prefer getting things done and being in control.
- May be insensitive.

THINKING

INTROVERSION ← → EXTROVERSION

- Focused on helping, harmony, and one-on-one relationships.
- Prefer being calm and patient.
- May not share feelings until it is too late.

- People-focused, social, entertaining.
- Prefer attention and lots of interaction.
- May be dramatic and emotional.

FEELING

INTROVERTED FEELERS

EXTROVERTED FEELERS

By understanding your own personality style, you can predict your behaviors in certain situations and better understand what you need from others. With a preference for extroverted thinking, I love getting things done and can easily focus on tasks. I occasionally step on others' toes because I focus on facts and not on how others are going to feel about an issue. I don't mind conflict and don't hold a grudge if someone is angry with me. I'm also fairly independent and don't collaborate particularly well with other people.

By being aware of your personality style, you can also predict what others will experience from you. Ultimately, as we will discuss in the Developing Relationships section, if you understand another person's personality style, you should be able to adapt your approach to be more effective and influential. If I am trying to influence introverted feelers, I will not put them on the spot; I may instead send them a few questions to consider ahead of time so they have time to think through the issue. I will check in on how they are feeling and will not mistake their quiet for agreement (or compliance). I will also ask for their help because they love helping!

I am often asked is there a "perfect" personality style for a particular job. For example, in outside sales, managers may want someone with an extroverted feeling style because they tend to be good at building lots of casual relationships and enjoy people. However, what if the outside sales job requires a high degree of detail orientation and planning? Perhaps someone with an introverted thinking style would be more successful. No matter the job, there is no one style that can be successful; we all have the ability to adapt our approach to a given situation, even if we have a preference or a default style.

We all have the ability to adapt.

VALUES

As one of the main constructs of Values Based Leadership, understanding what you value is an essential part of Building Awareness. Most of us believe we know what we value, even though we haven't taken the time to reflect on these fundamental aspects of our personality. Not all of our values are obvious; they can be subtle and just beyond our awareness.

The best clues to what we really value are the strong emotional reactions we experience. When you experience positive emotions, for example, if something makes you happy, chances are one of your core values was met. If we value hard work and someone compliments us on how much effort we put into our job, we will feel good. If we value financial security and someone asks us how to save money, we will probably be inspired. Negative emotions are the opposite. When we are angry or upset, chances are someone violated one of our values. For example, if you value freedom and someone tries to control you, you are likely to feel upset. If you value collaboration and someone leaves you out, you may feel hurt.

Neuroscience backs up this observation. In a recent study at the University of Southern California, the brains of participants who shared a story about their cherished values lit up brain scans more than stories that were not based on their values. There have been other neuroimaging studies mapping out values-related behaviors, rewards, goals, and decision making. Even though we don't fully understand the biological mechanism, values clearly have a significant impact on how our brains respond to stimuli. While we continue to deepen our understanding of how our brains evolve, there is also a clear line of research on how we form our values.

Consider this: when you were a baby, then a toddler, you observed the world, especially the example set by your parents. Think about the house you grew up in—what were you praised for? What were you punished for? Your family system—the collection of inter-personal dynamics that evolved between your parents, siblings, and close relatives—shaped you from a young age. As you grew, you interacted with more people, experienced more situations, and began to form assumptions about how the world works. You saw more models, behaved in more ways, and began to form your own identity and belief system. Over time, experience hardwired those beliefs into your brain; those beliefs ultimately became your core values. Stable and enduring, these neuroconnections influence how you respond to situations, how you feel about the world, and how you behave. Since you are wired for values, it makes these choices difficult to change because they are not just random but part of a biological superhighway.

The first technique for understanding what you value is to think about when you are at your best and feel the most energized. Again, given the connection between values and emotions, that energy you feel is tied closely to what is at your core. Then consider when you are at your worst and feel the most de-energized and frustrated. Like what energizes you, the things that sap you are clues to what you value most (or don't value, in this case).

BEST TOOL?

At InnerWill, we prefer instruments that have been rigorously tested and validated over time based on real research, yet assessments are often proprietary and reliable data can be difficult to find. Like many of our approaches, we believe individuals should be ruthlessly pragmatic about the tools they use. If they work for you, and your situation, use them. If they don't work, don't.

Another way to discover what you value is to reflect on where you spend your time, your money, and your energy. Values drive behaviors, and your actions likely reflect these deeply held beliefs. Some people keep track of their time using a calendar or journal, then look back after a week or a month to discover how they really spent their time. You may look at your credit card statement to see where you spend your money or your bank account to keep track of your savings. As for energy, pay attention to what you pour yourself into, where you spend most of your effort, your preparation, and even your fretting and anxiety. You have limited time, money, and energy, and you are spending it for a reason. Your core values lie at the heart of those choices.

Another technique for discovering what you value is getting feedback from others. Asking them what they believe you value can help you look in the mirror. Others may see you more clearly than you see yourself, especially if a value is subtle or in your blind spot. This technique may be challenging because others' interpretation of your behavior is run through their own filters. Their interpretations of your values may not be accurate yet are great data points to use to build awareness. Keep in mind: we judge ourselves on our intentions, while others judge us on our behaviors. They can see only the outside of the house.

Typical leadership workshops and coaching programs have you choose your values off a list, and that's where the work stops. A better practice is first to reflect on how your values were formed through the significant events in your life. Next, it is crucial to examine how they shape your decisions, behaviors, and relationships. Finally, you define your values as clearly as you can, using words that resonate with you (after all, they are your values, not your mom's, not your pastor's, and not your manager's). Part of that definition is identifying how to put your values into action so you can easily determine when you are acting on them and when you are not. The format looks like this:

VALUE
Definition
Behavior 1 Behavior 2 Behavior 3

Let's say you value integrity. Integrity can mean a wide variety of things to a wide variety of people, so you will want to define what it means to you. For example, let's say that you believe that integrity is all about doing the right thing, whether or not someone tells you to do so. So you define integrity like so:

Value: Integrity

Definition: Doing the right thing when no one is looking

Next, you will want to consider what your value looks like in action. What are some simple behaviors that illustrate the value that you can act on every day based on your definition? For you, doing the right thing when no one is looking means being honest with other people, thinking through the ethical choices in a situation, and building long-term, trusting relationships with others. And so, you identify three straightforward behaviors that support your definition:

Value: Integrity

Definition: Doing the right thing when no one is looking

Behavior 1: Be honest.

Behavior 2: Consider the right thing to do in every situation.

Behavior 3: Build trust with others.

I'm a fan of focusing on a few core values that you act on at work and home that are always on, that guide you in every aspect of your life. It is helpful to focus on no more than five core values and three supporting behaviors. Why just five? In my experience, we believe we value lots of things, but a small handful of values actually influence our emotions and actions.

Again, the format looks like this:

VALUE 1	VALUE 2	VALUE 3	VALUE 4	VALUE 5
Definition	Definition	Definition	Definition	Definition
Behavior 1	Behavior 1	Behavior 1	Behavior 1	Behavior 1
Behavior 2	Behavior 2	Behavior 2	Behavior 2	Behavior 2
Behavior 3	Behavior 3	Behavior 3	Behavior 3	Behavior 3

Thinking through and defining your values and behaviors gives you clarity about what matters; it also makes it easier for you to make difficult decisions that align with your values. Plus, if you choose to communicate your values to other people—like your family or your teams at work—your definitions can help others see what's important to you and support your accountability to those values.

BELIEFS AND ASSUMPTIONS

Beliefs can be tricky: they may help us succeed, such as a student who believes she is smart and goes on to get straight As. Beliefs may also be limiting, such as another student who believes he is stupid and drops out of school. Our beliefs underpin our values, like believing that honesty is the best policy and developing the value of integrity. Beliefs can lurk below our awareness. They are at the bottom of the house because we are likely only dimly aware of them and they may only be revealed through long years of reflection and study.

ASSUMPTIONS **BELIEFS** **VALUES**

Beliefs—and assumptions—can also have a shadow side, as they can be the fears that sabotage us and hold us back. I value hard work, and it's almost always my answer for the problems I face. Having trouble reaching a sales goal? No problem, just work harder. The assumption is that if I fail, it is because I did not work hard enough. My fear in this case is that if I don't work hard enough, I will be doomed, probably forever, and that others will no longer respect me. It might sound crazy to say out loud, but our fears can be pretty irrational. Thousands more people die from bee stings every year than are eaten by sharks, but which are you more frightened of? Don't even get me started on spiders.

You probably have your own version of beliefs, assumptions, and fears that influence you. Value relationships? You may assume that being liked is the only way to be successful, and if people don't like you, it will be the end of the world (it won't be...probably). Value independence? You may assume that if anyone tells you what to do, they are trying to control you and limit your freedom. You might be afraid that you will never stand on your own

two feet if you give up control for a second (not going to happen...
most likely). Value harmony? You might assume that everyone
must be happy all the time. And if they are not happy, they will
take it out on you for the rest of your life (depends on the person...
just kidding, but just in case, make sure no one ever feels bad).

Understanding your beliefs is a fairly challenging and advanced
form of self-awareness. Unlike our values and personality styles,
beliefs are tougher to figure out because they are buried deeper
than other parts of our psychology. Yet, they are the foundation
of the house.

One technique to understand our beliefs is to pay attention to
our emotions and that voice in our head whispering why we can
or cannot do something. Our internal monologue has unfiltered
clues about our beliefs and assumptions. It might be the voice of
another person in our head or our own insecurities trying to get
our attention. That voice can be helpful, like the voice of Jiminy
Cricket on Pinocchio's shoulder. That voice can also be unhelpful, especially when it tears us down and limits us. Practicing
Reflection, another of the five VBL practices, can be a great tool
for seeing those underpinning assumptions more clearly as well
as how they influence our behaviors.

IDENTIFYING STRENGTHS AND WEAKNESSES

We all have things that we excel at, that come easy to us, that
we are naturally built to do. Other skills take consistent practice
over time, and we develop them through effort, the right coaches,
and tons of feedback. Our strengths—whether they came to us
naturally, or if we developed them over time, or both—are what

we lean on to accomplish tasks and get through life. Our strengths may be obvious—like an actor's charisma or an athlete's skills—or they may be hidden and only revealed by circumstance, such as when we discover we really do have an affinity for math.

Our weaknesses are similar. They are often the activities we engage in that are not natural to us, that feel clunky or awkward when we attempt them. They are the actions we avoid if given the choice. Our performance in these areas would never be described as strong, or perfect, or even okay. Our weaknesses may be obvious to us and hidden from others, or others may see them clearly while those weaknesses remain stubbornly rooted in our blind spot. It has taken me years to realize that I excel at adapting in the moment and that I am a strong long-range planner, although I can't tell you what I am doing next week. If I ever lose my calendar, then I may as well have a seat and wait for someone to save me.

Our weaknesses may also be our overused strengths. For example, let's say you are a very honest person. Honesty has always served you well, but occasionally you will hurt others with your searingly direct comments. In this case, you are overusing your strength of honesty. There can be a dark side to our strengths, just as our weaknesses may have positive attributes. For example, my inability to remember song lyrics fuels my creative substitution of new words, much to my wife's annoyance.

Identifying your strengths and weaknesses is relatively straightforward. We have all received numerous grades, performance reviews, sports scores, and other data that can point out what we are good at and what we are not. Taking time to reflect on all this data should indicate the obvious strengths and weaknesses we have—again, using the fifth practice of VBL.

To keep it simple, ask others for feedback directly. Want to get a snapshot of how you are doing as a human being? Ask your kids. Then ask your friends. Then ask your family members, especially the honest ones. They will provide you with plenty of data about your strengths and weaknesses, although my 90-year-old grandmother still refers to me as her special boy and I'm no longer sure she can be trusted.

Once we understand our strengths and weaknesses, the question becomes this: what do we do with them?

Remember that everyone has strengths and weaknesses; we are all imperfect beings who have amazing gifts. We can learn and grow by developing skills and strengthening our natural abilities. We can learn new knowledge, adding technical skills and techniques. We can learn more than new skills; we can transform the way we think about the world and how we go about interacting with it. Our brains continue to make connections until we die; even if we lose a few brain cells along the way, learning does not stop once we are adults.

There are several schools of thought about our development. Classically, we focus on improving the things we are not good at—strengthening our weaknesses. Gaining technical knowledge and skills has been the focus of our education and our leadership development. However, there is a growing movement focused on developing our capacity to see the world in new ways and transforming how we think. From the world of positive psychology, there is a relatively new idea that we should focus on leveraging our strengths, not ignoring our weaknesses but also not investing time and energy into closing those gaps in our skills.

Be ruthlessly pragmatic about your strengths and weaknesses. If it works for you to focus on your strengths, great. If it's better for you to focus on your weaknesses, great. If something isn't working for you, try something else. We are the greatest experiment of our lives, and there is no one right path to become the best version of ourselves.

The intent of Building Awareness is to see ourselves clearly—accepting that we have strengths and weaknesses and still moving forward.

SEEKING OUT FEEDBACK

Our behaviors impact other people every day, whether we are aware of the impact or not. Formal leaders have an even greater impact on others, as they often hold powerful influence tools: continued employment, compensation, job assignments, and task delegation. Understanding how our choices impact others is a key aspect of seeing ourselves clearly; we may not intend to hurt someone through our actions but do so without realizing it. We may intend to inspire but leave them confused instead. We may not even think about others at all and be surprised that we have the impact we do. The only way to know how we impact others is through feedback.

For example, let's say I've had a bad day at work. I come in the house, a cloud above my head, and glare at my wife. Not because she did anything, but because I'm tired and angry. My wife may react to my anger by asking herself, "I wonder what happened? I wonder what I did?" She may also think, "How dare he come in the house angry. Doesn't he know I've had a bad day? It isn't fair! He's so inconsiderate of my feelings." She grows angry, and we both spend the rest of the evening glaring at each other and the kids. The dog, however, is oblivious. He does not assume that he is the cause of my bad day and believes that time in the yard and a good chew toy can fix anything.

Or let's say you are quiet and distracted throughout a meeting. You barely say a word and do not contribute to the discussion. You don't notice your boss growing irritated. After the meeting, she pulls you aside and asks why you don't care about the project. Her question leaves you confused and flustered; you didn't realize that by being quiet, you left her feeling aggravated at you.

There are many behaviors we engage in that can impact others in a positive way or can leave them feeling unappreciated and uninspired. Listening is a common challenge: when we don't listen to others, we leave them feeling unvalued. When we really listen to them, they often feel heard and understood. Communication is another opportunity for many leaders: we often share too little or in the wrong manner, leaving others feeling uninformed or confused. Perhaps we didn't have time to communicate well, or we didn't think to communicate, or even chose not to share any information. Regardless of our intent, it was unlikely that our goal was to create confusion or a lack of clarity. We are more likely to achieve the outcomes we want when we seek out feedback. As Greg McCann, family business consultant, former college professor, and executive coach puts it, "Leading without feedback is like driving home with the dashboard covered."

When we understand our impact on others through feedback, it gives us the opportunity to make a more informed, more conscious choice. The Five Practices of Values Based Leadership help us make intentional choices that lead us to the outcomes we want to achieve. As human beings, the vast majority of our choices are unconscious: we spend a great deal of time on autopilot. For example, have you ever left your house, driven for several miles, pulled into a parking lot, and suddenly realize you have no memory of how you got there? Driving is the most complicated thing most of us do, and yet, we can do it almost without thinking. Not safely or well, but we can do it.

When we are working with others, we often engage in the same sort of unconscious behaviors. For example, if we are typically sarcastic, we don't think through that biting comment about a coworker; it just falls out of our mouth. In the moment, we don't consciously consider that our sarcasm might impact others. Trust me, it does.

Acknowledging our impact on others is more than just being aware of our impact. Acknowledging means that we accept responsibility for our impact and that we understand the link between our behaviors and the results. Stephen Covey, discussing

Viktor Frankl, famously said, "Between stimulus and response there is a space. In that space is our power to choose our response. In our response lies our growth and our freedom." By acknowledging the impact of our behaviors on others, we have the chance to choose our response. It begins with reflecting on what impact we want to achieve. Do we want others to feel inspired? Appreciated? Clear about our expectations? Then we can see the gap between how they are feeling and how we would like them to feel, then adjust our response. Or we may find that we have the impact we want to have on others and need to make similar choices in the future.

Feedback comes in many forms. Sometimes it is formal, such as when a boss pulls us aside and says, "May I give you some feedback?" Sometimes it is informal, such as when our spouse complains that we left dishes in the sink again. Sometimes we receive it through numbers, like the score on a scoreboard or the sales figure for the month.

Our reaction to feedback depends on a number of factors, many of which make it less likely we are able to hear and then act on it:

- If it does not fit with our self-perception, we may ignore it.
- The less we like the person who is delivering it, the less able we are to hear their feedback.
- The less the feedback aligns with our goals, the less able we are to pay attention to the feedback.
- The more subjective the feedback, the less likely we are to listen to it.

Feedback is the root of understanding who we are and the impact we have on other people. Feedback is a great teacher when we see it that way. However, feedback is just data, data we can use in service to our goals. We pay attention to some of the data and ignore other parts of the data. Learning what to pay attention to and what to ignore is key. Feedback that serves your goals is the kind of data we should pay attention to, no matter the source. Learning how to learn from people we don't like is a skill that is an important part of our development.

Feedback is data we can use in service to our goals.

Research tells us that feedback focuses our attention. That focus sometimes helps us and sometimes hurts us because we have only so much attention to go around. It is better to seek feedback rather than wait for it since we can make sure we get the data we need and really want. We are also programmed to avoid anxiety and be okay, which means we may ignore the crucial feedback we need because it makes us uncomfortable. The better we can grow the skill of seeking feedback, really hearing it, keeping what's useful to us and discarding what's not, the better we can develop as leaders. The more feedback we get, the less likely it is that feedback will hijack our emotions and leave us sad, angry, or dejected. It moves from a dramatic event to just another Tuesday.

Building Awareness—understanding who we are and the impact we have—is a key part of leadership. There are many ways to build our awareness, whether through reflection and feedback, formal assessments, or conversations with others. Our awareness is helpful because it gives us the information we need to choose—to choose what behavior will most likely help us achieve our goals and have the impact we want to have.

Twenty years ago, when I looked in the mirror, I saw a laid-back surfer. Today, not so much. When you look in the mirror, what do you see?

KEY TAKEAWAYS

There are three ways we can practice Building Awareness:

1. Examining our values, style, and beliefs
2. Identifying our strengths and weaknesses
3. Seeking out feedback

By building our awareness, we can see ourselves more clearly and identify the impact we have on others.

FEEDBACK IN REAL LIFE

I was getting frustrated with the project team I was leading—we weren't making enough progress, and I let the team know how irritated I was. Much to my surprise, the team told me that I was the reason we weren't making progress, and the example they gave was that we just spent 45 minutes talking about my frustrations instead of getting work done. In that moment, it hit me that rather than blaming them, I needed to take responsibility for the impact I was having on the team. It was a tough but important moment for me.

—SHARON AMOSS, INNERWILL

A STORY ABOUT REALIZING POTENTIAL

My first wife died when I was 42 years old and my life changed forever. I remember coming back from her funeral to our wonderful home filled with nice things on a golf course and thinking, "Is this it—all there is?" We had been so focused on our careers, on achieving, that we had put off having children until we couldn't. After she got sick, I was busy taking care of her and my career; I only took vacation to care for her and worked extra days so I could be with her during her treatments. I never missed a day and seldom missed a deadline. My wife was the same way. We were both successful but not significant. Now alone in that wonderful house full of things on the golf course, I had to find a way to go on without her, to build a life that did not feel so empty—a life with purpose! I needed to figure out what was going to be significant in my life.

As I read books, reflected, and prayed, I realized that my purpose was to make a significant positive difference in the lives of others. I took out a piece of paper and drew a triangle—the delta symbol—and added a plus sign in the middle. That's it; that was my purpose. I carried that paper in my pocket to remind me, "This is why I am here and what I'm here to accomplish."

My purpose has changed slightly now that I am semi-retired. I am blessed with a wonderful family and life. My purpose is still to make a positive difference, but now I "influence committed others to become the best version of themselves." The choice I made after my wife died changed the way I view the world and is hopefully helping a few others along life's journey.

—JAY COFFMAN, FORMER VICE-PRESIDENT, LUCK
COMPANIES, VALUES BASED LEADERSHIP COACH

CHAPTER 5

Realizing Potential

Why does Realizing Potential matter?

On our leadership development journey, we need to know where we are going, who we want to become, and what impact we want to have in the future.

Maggie Mistal, a career coach, uses a simple model when helping individuals find the job they want. She describes the process as "soul search, research, job search." The model assumes that in order to find a job where we can thrive and do our best work, we must first start by understanding who we are and what we really want. Building Awareness goes a long way to helping us soul search and seeing ourselves clearly. Realizing Potential is about describing not just who we are today, but who we want to be. It is about looking into the future and describing what we hope to come true. In many ways, it is about creating a self-fulfilling prophecy: if we describe it and act on it again and again and again, we can make that prophecy come true. Over time, we can develop our best selves.

> *"Soul search, research, job search."*
>
> —MAGGIE MISTAL, CAREER COACH

There are three ways of Realizing Potential:

1. Discovering our purpose
2. Developing our best self
3. Pursuing ideal environments

DISCOVERING OUR PURPOSE

Purpose is a big, heavy word. It describes why we are here, why we walk the earth, what our big reason for existing is. When thought about in those terms, it is no wonder it can seem overwhelming to contemplate. Aaron Hurst, in his book *The Purpose Economy*, describes a future where more and more organizations and individuals promote the idea of purpose. And not purpose as in the big reason for existence but purpose as a verb, as in something we do.

Purpose does not have to be big and heavy (although it can be). Purpose is your why—why you do what you do. It's a North Star to help you navigate between the shoals, a reason to get back up when you get knocked down, a call to do and be. Purpose is a reason for being and a statement of intent.

My purpose, for example, is to be a great dad, to be a great husband, and to lead and develop people. It's not the most awe-inspiring purpose ever; I'm not going to save the world or anything, but I am going to be there for my kids and try to raise them as fundamentally decent human beings. I am going to be a good partner for my wife—the strong independent woman that she is—and build our life together. And I am going to spend my days helping others be amazing, no matter what my actual job title is. My purpose provides clarity for me and my actions. It reminds me of what is important. It's not a finish line to cross, although when I get to the end of my life, if I have done those three things, I will feel that it is a life well lived. Your purpose, your why, needs to be compelling enough that it provides fuel for you each day. It should be unique to your strengths and a calling to improve. It should be worthy of your time and effort. We have, on average, 22,000 days to spend on this earth as adults, and your purpose should be a good use of the majority of those days. As Guy Clumpner says, "No one ever gets to his deathbed and says, 'Please bring all my stuff to me so I can see it one more time before I go.'"

When you consider your purpose, it is sometimes helpful to consider it from multiple angles. You might ask yourself, "What energizes me?" or "What impact do I want to have at work, at home, or in my community?" You may look back through your life and consider the themes that you have always lived by. You might consider your future and how you want to spend your time, money, and energy.

Another aspect to consider when describing your purpose are your values. How do those deeply held beliefs shape your why? For example, I value "framily"—my closest friends and family—a value that shapes my purpose of being a great dad and husband. I also believe in people's fundamental goodness and their ability to grow and develop, hence my desire to develop others. Finally, I believe in leadership and its power to make a significant positive impact on the world. Therefore, spending my life leading others is instrumental to who I am as a person. If others describe me as a great dad, husband, leader, and developer of people, then I must be doing something right.

IMPACT

Another part of our purpose is to define what impact you want to have on others. Do you want to inspire, motivate, or help build their confidence? Do you want to coach or mentor? Many of us feel blessed in our lives and want to somehow return those blessings to others. The thinking goes, "Once I am finished with my career and my kids are grown and I have more time, then I will give back." Or you could live your life in a way right now that aligns with your long-term vision of returning blessings to others. You impact others every day through your actions, whether you realize it or not. Why not be intentional about it? Like compound interest on a savings account, the choices you make in the moment can add up to a huge impact over time.

Sometimes I am plagued by an irrational fear that I am wasting my life and that somehow I will get to the end and feel like I failed. It gives me a feeling of dread and worry that I should be doing more, accomplishing more, or that somehow I turned right when I should have turned left. Of course, it's only fear talking—the same fear linked to my beliefs about achievement and my value of hard work. The solution to my fears is to remember my purpose and to focus on the impact I have on others. That's it. And if I do get to the end and I have made a positive difference in the lives of others, then it will have been worth it. Many of us are hungry for meaningful work and meaningful lives. We have the opportunity to infuse whatever we are doing with meaning in purpose. Again, it is a choice to live and work on purpose, with purpose.

> "No one ever gets to his deathbed and says, 'Please bring all of my stuff to me so I can see it one more time before I go.'"
>
> —GUY CLUMPNER, PRESIDENT, HOLT DEVELOPMENT SERVICES

DEVELOPING YOUR BEST SELF

Once you understand your purpose and have considered the impact you want to make on others, it's time to discover your limits, then surpass them. We call this developing your best self. It's about becoming the best version of yourself at work, at home, in the community, in your place of worship, wherever you go. It is based on the idea that there is no one right way to be. No perfect personality, no perfect set of values, no perfect set of skills but using what's natural to you and building on it.

Recently, there has been a lot written on the power of introverts—to lead, to hold positions of influence, to help move the world. We once thought you needed to have a tuxedo and a microphone to lead. You had to be charismatic, larger than life, and outgoing to be a great leader. You could lead on charm alone. We have come to realize that it takes more than charisma to lead. If you are an introvert, be the best introvert you can be. For example, Gandhi felt he needed to be more comfortable addressing people, first in a courtroom and then in the wider public. He studied how to speak up, network, build relationships, and lead with a vision.

If you are an extrovert, learn how to be quiet, listen, be comfortable in silence, and ask questions instead of sharing an opinion. There is a just-right place for all of us to find. We are all works in progress, and our work is never done. If we work first on ourselves, that gives us the ability to model self-development for others so that they, too, are inspired to do the heavy lifting and hard work of developing their best selves.

To develop the best version of ourselves, first we describe the person we want to become. Imagine an idealized version of yourself in whatever role you aspire to, be it a CEO or a great mom or a great CEO mom. To describe your idealized self, you may answer some questions about the role or person you aspire to become. For example:

- How does a great CEO mom behave?
- What skills and competencies does she have?
- How does she impact others?
- What do other people say about her?

Going through an exercise like this can help you define what you aspire to become and help you see the difference between where you are today and where you want to be in the future.

Second, developing your best self requires understanding who you really are—by building your self-awareness. Looking in the mirror, seeing ourselves clearly, and accepting both our amazing strengths and our gaps is a challenge of courage and conviction. It takes courage to see ourselves clearly and the conviction that we can get better over time. We can increase our capacity over time—our capacity to lead, take on more, face challenges, deal with conflict—and as we build our capacity, we become the best version of ourselves. Developing our best selves is a choice—a choice to face the hard truth that we are not perfect beings but human beings.

For example, I value independence, strength, excellence, responsibility, and hard work. Living in alignment with these values has made me successful and created gaps in my leadership. I have had to learn how to collaborate with others: seeking their input, listening and validating their ideas, empowering them to make decisions. My independent nature drives me to stand on my own. Yet, depending on others is exactly what teamwork requires. I am also really bad at asking for help, which increases my workload and stress and gets me involved in projects best left to others. Like all of us, when I overuse my strengths, I am less effective.

Humans are complicated. We are a host of strengths, gaps, values, beliefs, assumptions, ego, and fears. These make working on ourselves a lifetime project. These also make it a difficult project because our brains are designed to make sure we are okay and that we avoid being uncomfortable. Our brains are happy when we don't change: the status quo is predictable, and it takes a lot of resources to rewire our brains for something different. Our brains evolved with one job: to keep us alive. Not to live up to our potential. Not to be amazing. But to survive and, secondarily, to make more people. That's why self-development is a choice: because our survival is not dependent on our growth as human beings. This means development can be a hard, unnatural, and long slog.

Many of us say something like, "I have always heard that I am not a good listener. I've never gotten better at it. I feel bad about it, but I just can't seem to improve." Insert whatever behavior others have told you to work on: you are too aggressive, you are not aggressive enough, you are too quiet, you talk too much, and so forth. This assumes that in some way, if you were to just master this one skill, you would be so much better.

They could be right.

Maybe, just maybe, if you did develop that one thing, your effectiveness would improve tenfold. But here's the thing. Do you want to improve that skill? Do you believe you can improve that skill? Is that skill tied directly to your goals?

If the skills other people have told you to work on do not support your goals, don't worry about them. You have plenty of other things to focus on. But if that skill—like listening—does support your personal goals, then you should work on it, whether it is one of your strengths or not. We all have gaps, and the consequences of not improving the skill may be too high to ignore. You might be tempted to give yourself a free pass and plenty of excuses about why you don't need to develop it. (Remember, your brain doesn't really want to change. It likes a free pass.) Ignoring our gaps is okay; it's the human condition. But if your chosen path, career, or relationships require a skill other than your natural talents, then you will likely need to work on that skill.

Working on ourselves means increasing our self-awareness, understanding our impact on others, and reflecting on what impact we want to make. It means adapting our behavior to meet the needs of others and the situation. It means getting feedback on how we are doing and relentlessly exploring our blind spots. It means developing the courage to act on our values, time and again, when it's easy and when it's tough. It means being mindful of our choices in the moment and over time.

According to learning theorists and developmental psychologists, what we work on falls into two categories: horizontal skills, like mastering a new job, and vertical skills, like working on our ability to cope with ambiguity and change. Horizontal skills are more technical in nature; vertical skills are more psychological in nature. Our organizations tend to focus on horizontal skills, whereas work as leaders depends on vertical skills. I can teach you to use a word processing program (horizontal), I can teach you how to construct a sentence (horizontal), I can teach you the rules of grammar (horizontal), but it will take a long time and a lot of work for you to believe you are a great writer and capable of crafting great works of art (vertical). Mastering horizontal skills is relatively straightforward: a good instructor, the right tools, and enough practice, and you can learn most things. Mastering vertical skills like being comfortable with ambiguity, developing empathy, or letting go of the need to control takes time and effort and is fraught with emotions, especially anxiety and discomfort. Most people bail out before they make much progress. Most organizations are not set up to develop these skills, which means we are on our own. (Coaches are a great resource for developing our vertical skills; of course, I'm a coach, so I'm biased.)

Horizontal development expands our competencies.

Vertical development expands our capacity.

Let's go back to someone who says, "I've always been told I'm a terrible listener. For years, I've tried to be a better listener and not been very successful. Why should I keep working on it?"

First fact: Listening will make you more effective, no matter the role.

Second fact: Listening and leadership go hand in hand. You can't do one without the other.

If you want to be a better leader, you have plenty of incentive to improve your listening. And listening is a 100 percent developable skill. So what holds you back from improving your listening?

- Does listening support your long-term goals and purpose?
- Do you believe, deep down, that becoming a better listener will make you more effective?

If you said no to either of these questions, then you now know why your listening has not improved. How about a couple more questions?

- What are your values?
- How do they prevent you from really hearing another person?

Let's say you value competence, which means you do not want to be wrong and means you are supposed to have the answers. Listening may mean that you are wrong. Listening may mean you don't have the answers. Therefore, it is psychologically safer not to listen. You have what Robert Kegan, a developmental psychologist who has done extensive work on our resistance to change, would describe as a competing commitment. That competing commitment, along with the fear and limiting beliefs that go with it, prevents you from changing.

Consider these questions:

- What are your competing commitments—what keeps you from really hearing another person?
- When you think of listening, what do you worry will happen if you slow down and take the time to really hear?

You may value efficiency and feel that it takes a long time and a lot of energy to hear others. Therefore, you would prefer to get the gist and move on, as opposed to leaving the other person feeling heard and understanding what they have to say. Maybe you are uncomfortable with emotions. Listening leads to emotions, which makes you uncomfortable, so best not to spend a lot of time listening to others. Maybe you are not curious about what others have to say or believe you know what they think and feel and see no need to ask questions.

Whatever the reason, if you regularly get feedback that you are not a good listener, there is probably a reason you have not learned that skill. Until you become aware of the reason and make conscious choices to rewire those beliefs, you will not become a better listener. You will not stumble into becoming a better listener by accident. And as far as I know, there is no better listening pill, as much as I wish there were. Once you do the work—developing from the inside out, as some describe it— then you will be able to develop the mechanics of good listening.

PURSUING IDEAL ENVIRONMENTS

Let's go back to Maggie Mistal's model of soul search, research, and job search. Certain environments bring out our best selves and are more conducive to our growth as leaders than others. For example, if you value excellence like I do, you will do better in an environment that encourages excellence. If you are an artist, you will be more likely to realize your potential in an environment that encourages your artistic side. Conversely, if you are an artist and you are surrounded by what my wife describes as the blue suits, people focused on efficiency, numbers, and doing things in a cold and analytical manner, you are less likely to fulfill your potential. And yet, if you are a spreadsheets kind of person, that environment will feel like an amazing place to do good work (and buy that blue suit you've been eyeing).

Environments can be jobs, they can be cultures, or they can be the people you surround yourself with. Environments can be as big as the city you live in and as small as your cubicle (or cab of your dozer, or seat in your car, or coffee shop you frequent). We can't always choose where we wind up (or the country we are deployed to), but when we can choose, why not maximize our chances of finding that just-right place that gives us the life fuel we need to be amazing? If we haven't surrounded ourselves with people who bring it out in us, why not find people who do? If the place we work doesn't fit our values and we grow smaller and smaller until we simply disappear, how does that help us be our best selves?

Pursuing ideal environments does not have to be all or nothing. It does not mean you have to quit your job, say goodbye to your friends, and leave on a 12-month around-the-world odyssey (although it might). It could mean small changes. Find a hobby you like with people you enjoy and spend an hour a week with them. Decorate your office to suit your dreams. Hang a new air freshener in the cab of your truck. Small things add up to big things, so don't settle for just okay.

How do you know you've found the ideal environment? First, check your emotions. Are you generally happy and satisfied? Or are you tipped over every day—emotionally hijacked, unhappy, and unsatisfied? Check the environment. Does it fit you? If not, there may be a better place for you.

Another way to think of your ideal environment is using the metaphor of a dance floor. Imagine a child going to a dance lesson. There are many kinds of dance: modern, tap, ballet, ballroom, swing, you name it. Now imagine that child has to choose which dance floor to go out on—one that is the best fit for their values, skills, and passions. When we say find your dance floor, we mean to find the kind of dance—or environment—that brings out your best.

There are things in our environment that bring out the best in us. Some people thrive in orderly, well-structured environments. Others thrive in chaos where change is the norm. Some like peaceful meditative spots, and others like rooms that sound like they are filled with sugar-drunk six-year-olds. Many of us want to be surrounded by those we trust and work closely and collaboratively on teams, while others are independent, go-it-alone types who do their best work solo.

Finding your dance floor, that place of comfort and challenge that helps you perform at your peak levels, is an important aspect of realizing your potential. If you spend your days in environments that drain you, with people who sap you, you will not reach your potential. It's hard to give up the safety of where you are now to try and find the place where you can thrive. We talk ourselves out of leaving people who are bad for us and rationalize it by saying we are okay over and over again, even if we are clearly not okay. Values Based Leadership is about making choices that will help us reach our potential—and sometimes those choices are the hardest we will ever make.

However, if you are on the right dance floor, you have a chance of discovering your limits. And with practice, perseverance, and choice, you can surpass those limits. Over time, we may outgrow our dance floor—we may move on from ballet to modern—but if we don't explore what's out there and if we get stuck on a dance floor that is not our own, we won't become what we could be.

Find your dance floor.

Realizing Potential draws on the other four practices of Values Based Leadership. To pursue our ideal environment, we must build the awareness to know what's important to us. If we have the courage to act and seek another job or a new set of relationships, we are investing in our future. If we practice reflection, we may discover what our purpose is and how to develop our best self. And ultimately, we can discover what impact we want to make on this world.

KEY TAKEAWAYS

There are three specific ways we can practice Realizing Potential:

1. Discovering our purpose
2. Developing our best self

3. Pursuing ideal environments

By exploring our purpose, best self, and ideal environments, we can determine the impact we want to have, the person we want to be, and the direction of our leadership journey.

A STORY ABOUT DEVELOPING RELATIONSHIPS

I've had a long line of people willing to hold up the mirror to me and occasionally hit me over the head with it. I've been told I can sometimes be overwhelming, creative to a level that makes me unemployable, and occasionally smug with a dash of arrogance. And that's from my friends and mentors. I like to say, "It's so sad that these people I know and love and respect are all wrong." But they're not, of course. Developing Relationships starts with me working on myself all these years.

Beyond that, if I want to develop relationships with others, I have to be agile. I'm naturally a good listener, and I try to connect with a bit of humor, but what I mostly do is pay attention. People are starved for it. They want to be seen and heard. They want to be understood. And when I need to communicate, I adapt to their communication styles. If I have to give tough feedback to someone who is a strong thinker, I'm blunt. If I have to give tough feedback to a strong feeler, I will ask for permission and do some role-playing. I adapt to the person while staying aligned with my values. Somebody once said to me that "if anyone else had said that to me, I would have punched them in the mouth." That's when I know I have been successful. I'll go to the gates of hell with somebody, but I'm not their mother or their babysitter. I'm here to help them do some stuff.

—GREG MCCANN, BOARD MEMBER, INNERWILL, AND
FOUNDER, MCCANN & ASSOCIATES

CHAPTER 6

Developing Relationships

Why does Developing Relationships matter?

Leadership is always about people, and our effectiveness depends on the strength of our relationships.

As much as it pains some of us, we are all in the people business. Until the robots take over, we are always engaged with another person, be it a customer or a coworker, a loved one or a stranger on the street. Relationships are the core of leadership because leadership means influencing other people to act. Our success in doing so depends on many factors. Sometimes position power is enough to bend others to our will. Sometimes being charismatic is enough; others will follow our vision because they like us. Sometimes we can reward others for doing what we want by paying them or recognizing them publicly.

In Values Based Leadership, one of our goals is building trust with others, and we can only do that by developing healthy relationships. In 100 polls on what makes an effective leader, trust will be at the top of 99 of them. Call it honesty, call it integrity, call it being real, but at the end of the day, we want to believe others. We want to believe they will do what they say they will do; we want to believe they are not lying to us; we want to trust they have our best interests at heart. When we break that covenant as formal leaders or organizations, something precious and powerful is lost.

As many have said, trust is built in a lifetime and lost in a second. Through our own choices, we can influence how much others trust us and how much we are able to influence their behaviors. So how do we develop relationships? Through three behaviors:

1. Understanding others' values, styles, and beliefs
2. Empathizing with others
3. Supporting the success of others

As you can see, this is not an end all be all list for how to develop relationships and build trust in others, but it captures the heart of doing so. We assume that you are a good person, that you are honest, and that you care about people. If these assumptions are incorrect, you will struggle with Values Based Leadership. Additionally, there is a whole body of research on trusting the competence of others—that they meet our expectations for doing a good job. As a messy human being, you are not perfect, and no one expects you to be. However, others do expect a certain amount of effort and knowledge from you. Fall short of these expectations, and most people will give you the benefit of the doubt for a time. Yet, once they stop giving you the benefit of the doubt, building trust with them will be a tough road to walk.

How can we build relationships, then, as good people who tell the truth, care about others, and are generally competent?

We are all in the people business.

UNDERSTAND OTHERS' VALUES, STYLES, AND BELIEFS

Emotional intelligence, according to author Daniel Goleman, includes two types of awareness: self-awareness and social awareness. Understanding others' values, styles, and beliefs is all about social awareness; it means picking up on their cues, observing their behaviors, and talking with them about what they think, feel, and need. We don't always have the luxury of getting to know people as deeply as we would like, so we may have to use a few brief interactions to inform our understanding of others. Most human beings, fortunately, are exceptional at picking up cues from other human beings. Unfortunately, we are often terrible at using that information effectively.

I like the metaphor of an empathy antenna.

Imagine that inside each of us is an antenna designed to pick up on the signals that other people are constantly putting out. (Modern brain research describes mirror neurons as one of the brain's structures that performs this role, in case you want to nerd out on some neuroscience journals.) For some of us, the gain on the antenna is turned way up: we seem to pick up on everything, especially the negative stuff. For others, the gain is turned way down and we may not even notice the basic social cues around us. Again, we have a choice: we can choose to pay more attention to the cues of those around us. It takes listening, observing, and reflection; mostly, it takes curiosity. We must care enough about others to notice their cues.

There is plenty to get in the way of our curiosity about others: primarily our own stuff, our own emotions, or our own challenges. We may not like these others, or we may not respect them, and we may not trust them. We may not see the need to care. However, if we want to build trust or influence, we must understand them. Curiosity is like the electric current that makes our empathy antennas work; without curiosity, we can only pick up on dead air. And we certainly aren't acting on their cues.

Our empathy antenna is like a superpower. It's like mind reading, in a way—without speaking, you have a lot of information about how someone feels. As an experiment, observe the next stranger you meet. You might notice his body language: is it calm and relaxed, or is it tense like a coiled spring? Listen to their tone of voice: is it clipped and intense like a hailstorm, or slow and languid like a stream? Based on a few seconds of observation, you can make assumptions about what that person is feeling and probably come up with a story about why they feel the way they do. You will probably be right on the first and wrong on the second.

In the corporate world, we call this the ability to read a room. You walk in and almost instantly know how a group is feeling. You pick up on the emotional undercurrent. If we pay attention, we have a chance to notice how they are feeling, but we can stay disconnected from their emotions. If we are not paying attention, we may get swept up in those emotions, which makes our ability to see them clearly much more difficult. Emotions, especially negative emotions, are contagious, and they can pass from person to person very quickly.

Think about someone you have known and cared about for a long time. You likely know exactly how they feel at any given moment because you are trained to look for certain cues that you have been reading and responding to for years. I first learned I had this superpower when my wife was pregnant with our first child. I could walk in the door and instantly know whether I should sneak back out or announce that I was home.

There are always cultural differences, of course; some cultures encourage looking one another in the eye, while other cultures consider it rude. There are also physical differences that may impact our ability to pick up on others' social cues. Our antenna is far from perfect, as our associations are often driven by our own unconscious biases. Yet, when pictures of faces are flashed at research subjects, they are universally able to categorize how people are feeling.

From a leadership perspective, our empathy antenna gives us the ability to recognize more than just feelings; it gives us the ability to understand another person's values, style, and beliefs. Using our empathy antenna this way is amplified by skills we can develop, no matter the strength of our natural talent.

Caring requires curiosity;
curiosity requires caring.

CURIOSITY AND THE POWER OF QUESTIONS

In order to understand another person's values, style, and beliefs, curiosity is always the first step, followed by paying attention to what your empathy antenna is telling you about what the person thinks, feels, or needs in a given situation. Questions are a powerful tool in our curiosity toolkit, and it is a tool leaders often neglect. Want to know what someone values? Ask.

As leaders, we can use questions in hundreds of ways.

- To get information: What are the results of that initiative?
- To align action: What steps should we take?

- To assess: How did we do?
- To convince: Given what I have shared, what choice will you make?
- To attack: What's wrong with you?

In this case, we are asking questions to help us understand others. If the person's awareness is high, you can ask direct questions such as, "What is your personality style?" or "What do you believe?" Many people have not considered these questions, and so we have to ask related, but less direct, questions. For example, ask, "What energizes you?" or "What upsets you?" or "How do you like others to communicate with you?"

Answers to questions like these tell us what someone values. These answers also give us clues about their personality style. Are they an extrovert or an introvert? Do they prefer making decisions using logic and facts, or do they prefer using emotions? Are they future-oriented or focused on the present? What do they believe about what is right and true in the world, and how do those beliefs guide their behaviors?

Asking questions assumes that we listen to the answers without judgment. In a study published in the *Journal of General Internal Medicine*, doctors were found to listen for an average of 11 seconds before interrupting their patients. Imagine your own listening at work or even at home. How long before you interrupt? How long before you zone out or check your phone? How long before you disagree or correct the other person or walk away? Listening is a critical skill in work and in life, and yet, we often fail to do so.

Why listen without judgment? The more we judge others—using

**GREG MCCANN, FOUNDER, MCCANN &
ASSOCIATES, ON RELATIONSHIPS**

Even if a person has hurt or wronged us, we still have to act on our values in a
relationship. That's when they really matter, after all—when things are hard.

our own internal scorecard of what is right and good—the more others close themselves off to us. It becomes unsafe to be authentic and transparent about who they really are. If we are busy judging, we miss vital information and create more distance between ourselves and the other person. Google has done some great research on psychological safety on teams: the safer a team feels to be real, make mistakes, and be honest, the higher they perform. The same applies to any relationship we have, be it a formal leadership relationship, a peer, or our spouse. If we want to build others' commitment and not just their compliance to a vision or task, we must make them feel safe and build trusting relationships with them.

EMPATHIZE WITH OTHERS

Empathy means understanding why people feel the way they do. It does not mean agreeing. It means understanding. To empathize, first we have to be curious about how other people are feeling, then seek to understand why. All without judgment. Even if we disagree. Even if we have our own emotional stuff going on. Empathy means validating what others are feeling and reflecting that back to them. It means being able to take another person's perspective and gain insight into what they are feeling and why they are feeling the way they do.

Here's what empathy looks like in action.

Let's say your significant other has had a terrible day at work. He had an argument with a coworker and got chewed out by the boss. When he gets home, he is tired and worn out and angry and a little embarrassed. As he tells you his story, you can:

1. Freak out that he is going to lose his job.
2. Keep glancing at your phone as he is telling his story.
3. Listen to him for a minute or two, then tell him what he needs to do.
4. Listen to him and, once he finishes, say, "It sounds like you had a hard day. That must have been tough."

When we look at this list, the answer is obvious (D—right?). But how often do we choose to empathize? Given that most of us are problem solvers by nature, if we do manage to listen, we will likely choose C. Solving the problem is an efficient way to fix his issue and move on. But he probably does not need advice. He probably needs to feel validated and understood. Not fixed. B is a great way to communicate that whatever is happening on your phone is more important than him. A is about you and your own fear. I am not saying that A, B, or C are always the wrong responses, but if we want to develop relationships with others, then we need to do much more of D than the other answers.

To empathize, name the person's emotion: "It sounds like you feel x."

Then validate that emotion: "That must be y."

For example, "It sounds like you had a great day. That must feel really good!" or "It sounds like you are frustrated. That must be irritating."

Even if you get the emotion wrong, it invites the other person to clarify how they are feeling, even if they are not sure. When you get it right, it can feel pretty good to the other person. When others recognize my own frustration or anger or fatigue and say so, I get a little inspirational bump because they understand me without judging or fixing or, most importantly, telling me I should feel differently. Want to strengthen your relationships at work and at home? Stop telling people how to feel and halve the amount of advice you give.

What if you are a person who is uncomfortable with the emotions of others? Or who believes emotions have no place in the workplace? Or who believes if we were more logical, then the world would be a better place? Do you need to empathize?

Yes, yes, you do. Not everyone is wired to be objective and logical. I would argue that even the most logical among us is still under the sway of a lot of emotions. Understanding those emotions is one of the keys to Developing Relationships. You might have to be uncomfortable for a while, until you see the value in understanding why others feel the way they do. As my friend Jay says, quoting Theodore Roosevelt, "They don't care what you know until they know that you care."

Additionally, research shows us that empathy has a variety of benefits. For example, physicians who show empathy toward their patients leave the patients feeling deeply understood and validated, which leads to higher levels of trust in the doctor and their recommendations. Empathy has also been shown to result in stronger relationships and pro-social behaviors, and it has been linked to an increase in moral and ethical behaviors. Research also shows us that empathetic leaders experience less stress and more positive emotions. An interesting finding in research on empathy also links increased empathy with better results in medical settings, customer service settings, and entrepreneurial settings where understanding customers is key. Empathy has also been shown to encourage empathetic behaviors in others. Want others to display more empathy, whether from your team members or your children? Start by leading with empathy yourself.

Want to strengthen your relationships?

Stop telling people how to feel and halve the amount of advice you give.

Don't believe me? That's okay. To quote my favorite theory of change: find something to like about it. If you do not work on empathizing with others as a skill, you will find it extremely difficult to develop relationships. There's no wiggle room on this one. I am a person who is logical, task-oriented, and not very in touch with his feelings. I often joke that my pump had a feeling once, but it turned out to be a heart attack, so everything turned out fine. I have had to learn a lot about feelings and how to deal with them. Without empathy, I could not write this book, much less be a great dad or husband or lead and develop people. When I get feedback these days, it tends to be about my ability to empathize, express emotions, and recognize and acknowledge the emotions of others. No one tells me that I should be more logical and analytical or that I should be a better problem solver. If you are like me, I am willing to bet no one gives you that feedback either.

SUPPORTING THE SUCCESS OF OTHERS

Adapting our behavior—making conscious choices about how we show up—is another key to Values Based Leadership. Why adapt to others? Isn't my goal to be authentic, to be true to myself?

Authenticity has been written about and studied by philosophers and social scientists for years, and like any rich topic, there is an academic disagreement about what it means to be authentic and what the impact of it is. In general, when we are true to ourselves, we are less anxious, more trusted, and more effective in relationships. Sometimes being authentic puts us at risk, especially in environments where we value different things than the norm (see the Taking Action chapter for more on this). Again, in general, research tells us it is better to be authentic than not. However, it takes a surprising amount of work to recognize who we really are and what is important to us. It takes understanding our values, style, and beliefs, why we walk this earth, and what impact we have on others. In short, it takes the Five Practices of VBL: Building Awareness, Realizing Potential, Developing Relationships, Taking Action, and Practicing Reflection.

But being our true selves is not enough to lead others. We have to be ourselves with skill. It's the difference between honesty and brutal honesty: the real you may be brutally honest, but brutal honesty is not very effective and can undermine your relationships. There are many ways to be honest, but to do so with skill is more effective than telling everyone you meet that their babies are ugly.

Our goal should be skilled authenticity—again, being the best version of ourselves, not the unpracticed version. Remember our goal: support the success of others. If we want to maximize this impact, we will need to adapt our approach because everyone is different and requires different things from us as leaders. The challenge is being true to ourselves while adapting to meet the needs of others.

If we understand a person's values, style, and beliefs and we empathize with them, we can adapt our approach to be more effective with them. We will be more effective with a task-oriented, direct person by being task-oriented and direct. We will be more effective with a person who is introverted and prefers harmony by communicating one-on-one and giving that person time to consider.

One of my values is excellence—I want to be good at what I do, and I want to do good work. Part of that value is hard work. I had a former boss who would occasionally call me at the end of the week as I was driving home and tell me that he appreciated how hard I was working. I knew what he was doing and he knew that I knew, and yet, every time he did so, it inspired me a little bit, much to my annoyance. Since our values are a biological superhighway to our emotions, it's no wonder that he was able to elicit that response from me because he knew what was important to me.

ADAPTING IS HARD

I've always worked with people like me: analytical, less emotional. My new management team puts personal connections first, which made me angry and judgmental. I remember telling a friend, "We're both speaking English, but somehow we are NOT understanding each other." The way I'd operated up to this point wasn't working, and something needed to change. I made a conscious effort to focus on more emotions. It can be frustrating and takes energy, but it helps us move forward as a team.

—THERESE SMITH, CFO, HOMESTEAD BUILDING SYSTEMS

If you recognize another person for acting on their values, it can be a powerful inspirational tool. Let's say someone values accuracy, and you say, "I appreciate that your reports are always accurate to the third decimal place." This simple statement will give this person a little inspirational bump. If they also value adventure and you admire that sense of exploration, it will give this person another bump. All these little bumps of inspiration add up over time and strengthen that relationship. And stronger relationships make you more influential.

Supporting the success of others is not all rainbows and unicorns; it's more than just inspiration. Sometimes it means giving others the toughest feedback they have ever had in their lives. Sometimes it means making the tough decision. Sometimes it means holding others accountable and, if they work for us, firing them. Not because we are mean or have it in for them or want to hurt them, but because we care so much about them that we are unwilling to allow them to settle. Call it tough love, but we are trying to find that sweet spot, that just-right place between nurturing and challenging others to be their best.

Supporting the success of others does not mean completely giving ourselves over to the needs of others and ignoring our own. But it is about considering the impact of our behaviors, because there is always an impact. Sometimes that impact is modeling; remember, as leaders we are always onstage and serve as a powerful example of what to do and not to do for other people. Sometimes that impact is more direct, where our behaviors can help or hurt others.

Supporting the success of others means meeting them where they are. Let's say you need to influence a team to adopt a new process. The team doesn't understand the new system and wants to stick with the old one. They haven't tried it, but they have been burned before by systems that didn't live up to the promises made by overzealous project managers. They are skeptical that this new process will be anything but more work. You could command them to do it. Or you could promise them the moon. You could ignore the new process and make it someone else's problem.

Or you could meet them where they are by recognizing how they are feeling about this change. You could recognize the need to influence their thinking, to help them understand the features and benefits of the new system, and to clarify their understanding of what the system will do. You could provide them the right direction and support in trying the new system and encourage them along the way. As frustrating as it might be, it is always more effective to meet people where they are, not where we wish they were.

In this scenario, you did not get angry that they did not believe in the new system (that's about you). You did not ignore the issue (that's also about you). You did not hope they would just figure it out and get onboard (you) or make promises you did not know if the system could keep (you). You reflected on where they were in this change process, recognized they were a long way from acceptance, and stepped in to help them understand the system. You met them where they are. And by doing so, you built their commitment to the new process.

Meeting them where they are can feel frustrating, especially if we are already unhappy. We might be struggling to empathize with them, or because we are so upset and judgmental, we can't bring ourselves to be curious. However, if our goal is to influence their behavior and see a change, then adapting our approach is the only way to be successful. Wishing they were different is not a strategy for success.

Meeting them where they are may mean we settle for less movement than we'd like, or a slower process than we'd hoped for, or for an approach that feels awkward. Yet, developing relationships with people who don't trust us requires us to behave differently than we would with people we already have a great relationship with. Like any change, we have to go first. And building trust requires understanding others, empathizing with them, and supporting their success.

> Meet them where they are, not
> where we wish they were.

Developing Relationships is a choice. It means considering their values, style, and beliefs. It means understanding how they are feeling by empathizing. It means acting toward them with positive intent and genuinely leaving them a little better than we found them. Helping them stand a little taller than smaller, helping their candle shine a little brighter. Want to be a better leader? Do this more.

KEY TAKEAWAYS

There are three specific ways we can practice Developing Relationships:

1. Understanding others' values, styles, and beliefs
2. Empathizing with others
3. Supporting the success of others

By developing relationships, we will grow more influential and more effective, while making a positive difference in the lives of others.

A STORY ABOUT TAKING ACTION

There have been points in my life where I found myself at a crossroads between an easy path and a difficult path. I value integrity, strength, courage, and wisdom. And when I reach those crossroads, I have a choice to make. Integrity without action is nothing, and it takes courage, strength, and wisdom to take the right action. The easy path might mean saying nothing, ignoring an ethical or legal problem. As I was once told by the head of HR, "Forget you saw anything." The easy path would mean that you get to continue working and providing for your family. The hard path may mean you lose a job, or have to move, or put your career at risk. But I can't say I value integrity and take the easy path. I've never regretted taking the difficult path and for taking a moral stand.

My grandmother helped raise me, and she always spoke her truth. She was never rude, she never shouted, but she had a moral backbone. I try to do the same. And if I lose a job because I did the right thing, then that's okay. I have to be a human being and a parent, and I have to live with myself. Besides, I used to be a forklift driver, and I can always go back to that.

—CHRIS YATES, BOARD MEMBER, INNERWILL, AND CHIEF
TALENT OFFICER, FORD MOTOR COMPANY

CHAPTER 7

Taking Action

Why does Taking Action matter?

Our leadership and impact on others are the sum of the choices we make. And some of those choices are hard.

Reflect on a time when you stood up for what you believed in, even though the cost was high. Maybe you stood up for yourself, or a friend, or a loved one. Maybe you stood on principle. Maybe you called out unethical behavior. Maybe you gave some tough feedback. How did it feel? Scary? Empowering?

When we take action, we lead with courage. We run toward the fire versus away from it. We do the hard thing because it is also the right thing. We stand up when others tell us to stand down. We act even when the personal cost is quite high. When we get knocked down, we get back up.

Taking Action requires three behaviors to be effective:

1. Making conscious choices
2. Acting with your values
3. Facing challenges

Taking Action does not always require us to charge in alone, willing to take on all comers. Sometimes it's as simple as making a few more conscious choices throughout the day, choices that align with who we want to be and the impact we want to have on others. The vast majority of our decisions are unconscious—few people consider how they are going to brush their teeth each day or the exact route to take to work. Consider what would happen if you made a few more conscious decisions each day that support your leadership goals. Now imagine this over the course of a lifetime. The current average age of mortality in the United States is around 79 years old—that's in the ballpark of 29,000 days on this earth. As we mentioned before, that gives us something on the order of 22,000 days as an adult to make choices about the impact we will have on those around us.

Conscious choices are another powerful tool in our development and in our leadership toolbox. Conscious choices seem simple, but acting on purpose with a purpose is a step many of us don't take.

When considering what choice to make, we use the metaphor of the pause button.

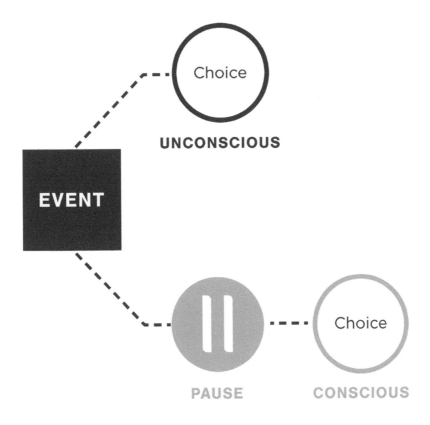

When an event happens, we make a choice whether we realize it or not. Author Viktor Frankl, in *Man's Search for Meaning*, argues that even in the most desperate circumstances—in this case, a Nazi concentration camp—that others cannot take away your power to choose how you respond to a situation. In Frankl's case, it was to respond to others with small acts of kindness and to take a stand, even though the stakes were high.

Most of us won't face the same horrors as Frankl, but we all have the same ability to choose how we respond to a given situation. Many of us are on autopilot: someone does something we don't like and we automatically get mad. Something happens that throws us off track and we get frustrated. Someone blows up at us and we retreat. We do so unconsciously based on how our brain is conditioned to respond over a lifetime of responses.

That unconscious response is our fight-or-flight response. Our brains evolved to keep us from getting eaten by bears. It is meant to be fast, not logical. When we get triggered by a bear in the woods or by getting cut off in traffic, the part of our brain responsible for emotional responses, our amygdala, goes into action. Our brain chemistry changes, which in turn triggers physical changes. Adrenaline floods our body, and cortisol increases how much sugar is in our bloodstream. Blood moves to our major muscle groups so we can fight harder or run faster. Our skin gets more rigid so we are more likely to survive an injury. Our vision narrows. This happens all before the parts of our brain responsible for logic, reason, and calculus even notice there is a bear about to eat us or a car about to hit us. We literally feel before we think.

Our fight-or-flight response happens in a few hundred milliseconds, yet we can consciously choose our behaviors if we are aware. We might not be able to head off what author Daniel Goleman calls the initial emotional hijack, but we can catch up to it. Imagine that something goes wrong—a customer snaps at us, for example. We could go into fight or flight mode, and either come out swinging or rush back to our corner. Or we could hit our pause button and mentally ask ourselves, "What is the most effective thing I can do in this situation?" then act on our assessment. Pausing gives the part of our brain responsible for logic a chance to catch up with the bear-fighting part of our brain.

Now imagine that you have given some thought to your purpose and the impact you want to have on others, both in the moment and over time. You have defined your values and understand your personality. And when you hit your pause button, you think, "What can I do in this moment that aligns with my values and my purpose?" then act on that assessment. With enough repetition and practice, it will get easier to make that choice. And with more choices, we are more likely to achieve the impact we want on others.

My friend Guy Clumpner loves to say, "Leadership is about what you do *before* you do what you do that matters." This is another great use for your pause button. Imagine you are walking into a tough meeting, where you know you will be emotionally hijacked by the people in the meeting or by the subject. You also know you want to have a positive impact on others. When you put your hand on the doorknob, before you walk in, hit your pause button and ask yourself, "How will I stay calm and present? What do I need to do to adapt my approach to be more effective? What's the most effective thing I can do on the other side of this door?"

Now consider what it's like to come home after a long, busy, stressful day. You put your hand on the doorknob, hit your pause button, and ask yourself, "How do I want to impact the people on the other side of this door?"

Pausing is not a lack of action; it is taking a moment to consciously choose our behavior.

> "Leadership is about what you do **before** you do what you do."
>
> —GUY CLUMPNER, PRESIDENT, HOLT DEVELOPMENT SERVICES

ACTING WITH YOUR VALUES

On the surface, it seems easy to act on our deepest held beliefs. If you value integrity, just be honest, right? What if you need to give tough feedback to your boss, who has a history of blowing up or turning the feedback gun back on you? What if that tough feedback could cost you your job and you are the breadwinner for your family? Not so easy.

Another example: What if you value family and a family member is taking advantage of you by borrowing money and not paying it back? Or a family member who does not want to get a job but wants to move in with you? Or a family member who gets drunk at every event and picks fights with you? How difficult would it be to watch them lose their house while you plan to kick her out of the next holiday party?

Acting with our values is easy when the stakes are low. I'm a hard worker, so it's easy to work hard. It's made me successful. I get rewarded for it. But what happens when that value of hard work leads me to work too many hours, travel too much, and not see my family, whom I also value?

Acting with our values is not as simple as it appears. It sometimes means taking a stand for what we believe in despite the cost.

More often, it means finding the just-right place between two opposite, interdependent values. In his work on polarity thinking, Barry Johnson describes polarity management as "both and thinking" where we don't have an either-or option. In our work lives, we need to focus on tasks and people. Focusing on one or the other will mean that we fail. Finding that just-right place is a difficult challenge all on its own.

Situations influence our behavior, along with our emotional responses to those situations. Remember Kurt Lewin's equation $B = f(P,E)$. Behavior is a function of the person and the environment. When we are in an emotional hijack because we are wrestling a bear, it is difficult to think clearly and logically about what we should decide. We feel before we think. The challenge increases when we don't have the skills or the practice we need to act with our values in tough situations. Being clear about what's important to us in those moments will help us act on our deepest held beliefs.

Acting with our values starts with Building Awareness. We need to understand what we value, state those values in a way that is meaningful to us, and describe what our values look like in action. Having clarity about our values will help us act on them in the moment and over time.

Next, we need to have worked on Realizing Potential, especially regarding what impact we want to have on others. Want to leave others inspired? We need to act on it in the moment. Want to be honest? We need to act on it in the moment. Whatever you decide is important to you should provide a helpful guide in determining your behavior in a given situation, much like a flowchart. If this happens, then I act this way.

Once we have identified our values, we need to define them in action and identify the behaviors that fit them. One person defines integrity as extra honesty, whereas another person defines it as acting consistently, whereas another person defines it as being authentic. They are all right, as long as it resonates with the person. Once we define our values and identify the behaviors, it's easier to know when we are acting in alignment with our core values and when we are not.

Practicing Reflection, the fifth practice of Values Based Leadership, can help us understand when we act on our values and when we do not. When we don't, there are probably similar conditions or situations that prevent us from doing so. When it comes to acting on opposite, interdependent values, there are probably fears and competing commitments at play.

For example:

You value honesty, which you define as being truthful to others.

AND

You value relationships, which you define as caring about other people.

You feel good when others feel good. But one of your friends is acting in a way you feel may hurt them in the long run. Maybe they are always late for events, or maybe they don't take responsibility for their mistakes, or maybe they unknowingly hurt others' feelings. You need to give them some tough feedback on their behavior that will not make them feel good. In this case, honesty and relationships are the two polarities and you want to act on both. How can you be both honest and focus on the relationship?

Robert Kegan and Lisa Laskow Lahey offer us one method for moving forward. In their book *Immunity to Change*, they describe the unspoken barriers that hold us back from acting on what we believe are our goals and suggest doing so through a series of small experiments.

As an experiment, you might:

· Look for five opportunities to give others positive feedback this week.

Or

· Give three people developmental feedback (also known as constructive criticism, or the not-so-easy stuff, or behaviors that need to change).

In the case of your friend, you may give them three pieces of positive feedback and one piece of developmental feedback. It's developmental because you have their best interests at heart and your feedback could help them grow. And it's an experiment to see if you can find the just-right place of both honesty and relationships.

There are times when I fail to live up to my values; we all do. For example, I value excellence, and when I get feedback that my work is not excellent and that I have fallen short, I take it hard. I recover, but I have a long moment of hurt, anger, and sometimes fear that I have failed. I will find myself, especially if I'm tired, allowing those negative thoughts to hijack my brain like some sort of old-timey train robber. A bunch of masked bandits jump aboard, and pretty soon I'm following the wrong track. I'm irritated and obsessed with what happened. When I allow those negative thoughts to hijack my brain, I'm less focused on my impact on others. I'm less able to empathize and care about others. I'm less aware of what's happening around me, and I'm less effective because I'm stuck inside my own head. In these moments, I may not even be aware that I am hijacked or that I am not honoring what's important to me.

In other cases, it's not that I fail to live up to my values but that I choose not to act on them. Let's say I value health but am uncomfortable with going to the gym. I'm busy, I work hard, I have a thousand things pulling on my time and energy, and going to the gym feels like one more thing to do; plus, it's something I am anxious about doing. Rather than find some other way to get exercise, I put it off while putting pounds on.

It is often said that courage is not the absence of fear but acting in spite of it. When we act with our values, research shows that others find us more trustworthy and are more willing to follow us; it makes us more effective as leaders and in our relationships. Especially when we articulate those values to others—saying out loud what we stand for—and then our actions match what we say. The audio matches the video; the walk matches the talk. If the stakes are high and the consequences are real, acting on those deepest held beliefs can be a gut-churning, sleep-depriving, anxiety-provoking situation. Especially when the world is telling us not to.

Want people to trust you?

The walk has to match the talk.

FACING CHALLENGES

When I was five, our house burned down in a matter of minutes. Everyone got out okay, but we lost everything. I can still remember being carried over my dad's shoulder, out of our kitchen and past our sandbox, watching the house get consumed by a hungry and angry fire. My dad's response to this tragedy was to become a volunteer firefighter. My brothers and I went with him on a few of these calls when we were young. Probably not the best idea to take a handful of high-energy, low-compliance kids to burning buildings, but we loved it. I was always struck that rather than retreating, rather than choosing to be anywhere but here, firefighters run toward danger, not away from it.

Facing challenges requires us to do something similar: run toward the fire versus away from it. Each of our fires may look different: some of our fires are the conflicts we are hoping to avoid. Some of our fires are the emotions we don't want to express. Some of our fires are facing our bosses or our coworkers or our customers. Some of our fires are that relative we don't like or that family event we are dreading. We all have people and events in our lives we'd rather not face. Facing challenges means we face those events because the fear of them is holding us back, not the person or the event. It's the voice in our head that is our enemy, not the people in our lives. And the only cure for fears like these is action.

HARD CHOICES

An internal client called me and said, "Fire her now." We had no facts, just anecdotes, so I said no. The client went around me to my boss, who promptly called me and said, "Fire her now." Again, I pushed back, knowing I might put our relationship and my job at risk. My boss reluctantly agreed to wait for me to gather the facts, which led us to fire the person. A few weeks later, our attorneys informed us she was suing for wrongful termination, which was ultimately dismissed, based on the facts. Leaning into your values may seem hard, but it always gives you strength in the end.

—WENDY BERENSON, INNERWILL

A caveat: There are real, honest-to-goodness evil people out there who mean us harm. There are events that will end with us getting hurt. Bad things happen to good people all the time. We will get in conflict with others, we will break relationships, and we may lose people on our journeys. And yet, for the most part, our anxieties are worse than the reality we face. Again, our brains evolved to make sure we stay alive long enough to make little people. I am convinced our positive, bright-and-sunny ancestors were eaten by bears. That left us, their descendants—worried, anxious, seeing bears where there are none—to carry on their legacy. As Charlie Luck, CEO of Luck Companies, likes to say, it's the eight pounds resting on our shoulders we have to worry about, not everything else.

How do we do it? How do we face the leadership challenges in our lives? The first step is recognizing those challenges. Our brains want to make sure we are okay. For example, how many times have you said, "I can't give my boss that feedback; it's not the right time"? Or, "Everything will be fine. If I do anything, it will make things worse." Or, "It's just not worth it." Secretly, we knew there was no right time and everything was not going to be fine.

We are exceptional at rationalizing our actions to ignore our fears. When we don't run toward the fire, we rarely think we are running away from the fire. We come up with reasons why running from the fire is the right thing to do. Sometimes running from the fire is the right thing. But often, it's just us playing it safe and settling for less than ideal outcomes. Leadership is a choice, and in those moments, we are choosing not to lead. It's okay; we all do it. What if in those moments we took a risk and we ran toward the fire? Could we save a few more people and keep the house from burning down in the first place?

When faced with a challenge—like a metaphorical bear in the woods—we should hit our pause button and ask, "What's the most effective thing I can do in this moment?" or "What choice aligns with my values?" Then choose. Consciously. That choice leads to an action, which hopefully leads us to the results we want both in the moment and over time.

That's it. Facing challenges mostly means facing our own fears, making a choice in spite of them, and accepting the consequences. There is no silver bullet, no way to become stronger or more powerful. But here's the funny thing: by acting with courage and facing challenges, we strengthen our ability to face future challenges. We build confidence and muscle memory every time we do so. Want to build courage? Make courageous decisions. Want to build confidence? Act as if you are already confident. Taking action is still the best cure for anxiety. Procrastination and rationalization are the cues to tell you when it's time to act. Putting off something you need to do because suddenly cleaning your kitchen is a pressing issue? Chances are, that's your brain avoiding feeling bad.

Part of facing challenges is dealing with failure. We have all failed—in school maybe we failed a test, in life maybe we let someone down or wound up divorced or lost a job. We make mistakes, we accidentally hurt the people we care most about, we make dumb decisions. Everyone fails from time to time. Sometimes life knocks us down. Sometimes through no fault of our own other than circumstance or bad luck or someone else's choices, we lose and sometimes we lose hard.

When we get knocked down and are lying on our backs, wondering what hit us, it's easy to blame others. It's easy to feel sorry for ourselves, to throw ourselves a giant pity party or even to be a victim. It's easy to make someone else the villain in our drama and wish that someone would ride in and save the day. However, when we get knocked down, the only solution is to get back up.

Resiliency has been studied closely over the past decade, with a few key findings. People who are resilient, who get back up after life knocks them down, who fail but who keep trying, believe that failure is not permanent. They don't believe they are bad for getting knocked down; they think they are good and worthy and have hope that the future will be better than the past. Resilient people don't internalize catastrophes or see themselves as a failure at life. Resilient people don't play the victim for long. (We all play the victim from time to time. No one is a perfect hero who always takes responsibility and never has a pity party.) The more resilient you are, the more successful you are. Resilient people get back up.

Facing challenges means nurturing our resilience so we can come back from failure as quickly as we can. To see failure as a learning opportunity or a chance for growth. We have the opportunity to conquer that little voice in our heads that says, "You're not good enough, or smart enough, or talented enough." Because you are. You just forget that fact from time to time.

> *"It's not the world, it's the eight pounds on your shoulders you have to worry about."*
>
> —CHARLIE LUCK, CEO, LUCK COMPANIES

Taking Action is a mix of awareness, choice, and courage that allows us to actively be the person we want to be. It is also the yardstick others will measure us by—they judge us by our actions, not our intentions. When others discuss you, what do you want them to say?

KEY TAKEAWAYS

There are three behaviors that make up the practice of Taking Action:

1. Making conscious choices
2. Acting with your values
3. Facing challenges

Making a few more conscious choices in alignment with our values will help us be more authentic and effective with others. To do so, however, takes both awareness and courage.

A STORY ABOUT PRACTICING REFLECTION

When I was 10, I started going to Alcoholics Anonymous meetings with my dad. He was in a community of grown-ups who were reflecting on the life they lived and taking an inventory using 12 steps. It helped me see that you can reflect, begin again each day, and recommit to the person you want to be. When I reflect, I'm practicing honesty with myself. It's one of the toughest things about a reflective practice—it's emotional, it requires me to be honest about how I feel and what I believe, and it invites me to stand on that foundation. I have to slow my process down, notice my biases and tendencies, and pay attention to how I see the world. I often ask myself, "What am I observing and what's my story about it? Have I put someone in a neat and tidy box, or have I looked with a second gaze, beyond what my critical mind might first see?" Over the years, my reflective practice has taken many forms. Today, I'm constantly reflecting whether I'm having a conversation or doing the dishes; I'm weaving back and forth as I try and see myself and the other more fully. That reflection has allowed me to have a more honest relationship with myself and others, where I can accept more of the goodness and beauty along with the blemishes and humanness. This work has allowed me to become more comfortable with all of it. It's helping me increase my capacity for love and being of service, even when service isn't easy.

—KELLY LEWIS, BOARD MEMBER, INNERWILL, AND A
FOUNDER AND PRINCIPAL, ANDIRON

CHAPTER 8

═══

Practicing Reflection

Why does Practicing Reflection matter?

How else will we learn from the past and apply those lessons in the future?

How often do we pause to learn? You probably think about what happened during the day, maybe on your ride home, maybe at home with your spouse or your friends, maybe in the middle of the night when you are trying to sleep but can't seem to turn your brain off. Just thinking about what happened during the day, and probably beating yourself up about it, is not enough.

Athletes, actors, and musicians record their performances and watch the tape. They look at their performance and make notes about what they can do to improve. Some organizations and military groups use an after-action report—a way to debrief what happened, what they learned, and how they want to apply those lessons in the future. This act of reflection—a pause before moving on to the next thing—gives us a chance to grow from our experiences. We can learn from our successes, we can learn from our mistakes, and we can learn from the example of others.

To get the most out of the lessons that life teaches us, there are three behaviors that make up Practicing Reflection:

1. Reviewing your thoughts, actions, and impact
2. Learning from experience
3. Applying the lessons

REVIEWING YOUR THOUGHTS, ACTIONS, AND IMPACT

Why review our thoughts, actions, and impact? First of all, our actions impact others, whether we recognize it or not. Our actions can lift others up, leaving them inspired and standing a bit taller, or we can knock them down, leaving them feeling hurt or more diminished than we found them. We don't have to end up in the principal's office to be reminded that our actions have consequences. The question is not just what impact do we *want* to have on other people, but what impact are we *actually having*?

Not only do our actions have an impact, but our thoughts do as well. Our thoughts and emotional responses to an event influence the choices we make, which influence the actions we take, which result in an impact. Our thoughts and resulting actions have an impact in the moment and over time. Remember, to realize our potential, our goal is to pause a little more and to make a few more conscious choices that align with the impact we want to have on others. Make those choices over a lifetime, and imagine the impact you could have.

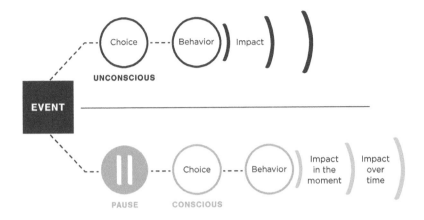

Our thoughts can be a source of emotional well-being. When my thinking grows negative and I think everything is terrible and everyone is evil and the universe has it in for me, that is a good sign that I'm burned out or tired or hungry. In these situations, my negative thoughts can spiral out of control. If I begin thinking about how bad something is, soon my mood matches those thoughts and I become angry because I allowed those thoughts to hijack my emotions.

When we review our thoughts, actions, and impact, we want to reflect on what is going on for us. In a mindfulness practice such as meditation, we might notice our thoughts and nonjudgmentally allow them to pass. Dr. Chris Reina, an expert on leadership and mindfulness, describes mindfulness this way: "Imagine you are an actor in a TV show, complete with dialogue and action and a plot. Now imagine that you are sitting on the couch, watching yourself act in this TV show. That's mindfulness, when we are able to step out of the TV and observe ourselves. We take ourselves out of the action, and that helps us be more present and not so tied up in our own ego and emotions."

In other cases, we may mentally discipline ourselves to stop our negative thinking. According to Dr. Jacques Dallaire, a performance coach who has worked with Formula One drivers and Special Operations units snipers, our conscious minds have a great deal of influence over our unconscious minds. Rather than focusing on all the things we can't control, he recommends that in the moment, we focus on what is under our control, including our thoughts. When you have a negative thought, Dallaire recommends redirecting it to something you can impact. Your mental dialogue in this case may sound like, "I am not going to dwell on this; I am going to think about something else." However we react to our thoughts, noticing is key because our actions soon follow.

When we focus too much on the things we can't control and we begin to feel stress, our view narrows. We begin to miss things in the wide view that may be incredibly important, like the second bear in the woods who also wants to eat us. One of the challenges we face in life is being able to narrow and widen our focus as needed and by choice. If we are not reviewing our thoughts, actions, and impact, we might not realize we are too narrow or too wide at the wrong times. And then we get eaten by a bear.

Charlie Luck uses this approach in his work as CEO of Luck Companies. "By being mindful and focusing on the things I can control, it allows me to take the right view when making decisions about our business. On some issues, I need to zoom in and focus on the details. On other issues, I need to have a wide field of view and see all the opportunities and threats in the environment so we can act strategically. If we aren't paying attention, we might miss things." Charlie, a former NASCAR driver and current Porsche GT3 Cup USA racer, uses this approach when he's racing. "Racing is a very precise sport...You have to know exactly when to accelerate, when to brake, how much to turn, how much pressure to apply to each of the pedals. If you're not 100 percent present, if you're focused on results or other drivers or anything but what you are doing at 120 miles per hour with two inches of clearance on either side, you are going to put the car into a wall and maybe get hurt."

These lessons apply not just to the racetrack but also to everyday life and business. According to Charlie, after each race, he reflects on:

A factors...the things I can control:

Did I have 100 percent focus, did I turn into the corner at the right place, did I apply the power at the right place? When my mind wandered, did I quickly refocus back on the track in front of me? The A factors will get you closer to the results you desire more than anything else. This is where our mental imagery and attention needs to be at the highest level.

B factors...the things I cannot control:

In the moment, quickly saying to myself, "That is a B factor" keeps me at the highest level of performance. It just started raining, a tire punctured, a caution flag happened when I did not want it. What competitors say about me, or what the crew will think about my choices. These are all B factors that draw your mind and energy away from performing well. Put the B factors in a box and close the lid. You need all your energy for the A factors.

Results:

Most of us overfocus on results. Did I win, where did I qualify, what was my lap time? Of course, we all want great results. Focusing on the result WILL NOT get you the result. Focusing on the result results in poorer performance. We get anxious, excited, upset, and all these distract us from the A factors—the very things that will get us the best results.

WAYS TO REVIEW OUR THOUGHTS, ACTIONS, AND IMPACT

There are many ways to review our thoughts, actions, and impact. Some people like to reflect on their drive home. Some like to reflect while they are doing an activity that does not need a lot of mental horsepower, like folding laundry or mowing the lawn. Dr. Reina says that he practices reflection by:

writing out "journey goals" for myself multiple times a week and especially before big events occur. These goals help remind me about what is important and what I hope to accomplish. When I write out these goals, it helps me begin with the end in mind so I can make these goals into reality, and it reminds me to enjoy the journey itself. I also practice reflection by periodically looking at my calendar to see if my energy is being committed mindfully. Am I committing my attention to the things that reinforce my values and encourage my growth and passions?

As you reflect, there are several questions that can help guide you:

1. What did you do? Did your actions align with your values? With your purpose?
2. What did you think and feel? (Remember, strong emotions reflect our deepest held values and give us insight into, well, us.)
3. What impact did you have? Did the impact align with what you want to achieve in the moment and over time?
4. How might you act more aligned with what you have identified as your purpose in life and your core values?

Some people love to journal as they consider these questions. Sit down with a piece of paper, or a computer, or a fancy spiral notebook and take notes on what happened. What did you do? How did you respond to others? Peter Senge, in his excellent book *The Fifth Discipline*, provides us with a great way to reflect in the moment. Split a piece of paper in half. What you are thinking goes on one side, and what was actually said goes on the other. It's a great way to map your ladder of inference, which is the process you go through in your head, often in a split second, that determines what you will do in a given situation based on your own filters, judgments, and emotions.

Another technique for journaling is simply to notice your thoughts, feelings, and actions throughout the day and describe them. Once you have amassed a few weeks of data, go through it looking for trends. It's a great way to build your skill of mindfulness, to notice what you are thinking and feeling at any given moment. By noticing our habits of mind, we can consciously choose our thoughts versus unconsciously allowing those thoughts to run roughshod over us.

Part of the value of journaling is that we have a written record of what happened. Why does it matter? Once we have insight about our habits of mind, or about our thoughts, feelings, and actions, our brains are pretty skilled at making us forget those insights, especially if those insights are threatening to our identity, cause us anxiety, or require us to change. Again, the eight pounds on our shoulders is what we should be worried about, not other people. We are good at having an aha about ourselves, then forgetting it five minutes later.

OTHER WAYS TO REFLECT

Some people keep a pad beside their bed so when they wake up in the middle of the night with a thought or a fear or a to-do, they can jot it down and go back to dreamland. I am not one of those people. If I start writing, I won't stop until daylight when I get up and go to work. I have a more extroverted method of reflecting: talking to other people and reflecting out loud. My brain works better when I engage with others who can help me sort through my thoughts and emotions and nonjudgmentally help me recognize my own thinking. Coaches are a great resource for this, as are people who nonjudgmentally listen and reflect what they hear. So often when we engage others, we try to solve their problems or tell them what they should do, or we tsk and harrumph and judge, but when we have really good listeners, they help us reflect.

Another way to review your thoughts, actions, and impact is to complete self-guided worksheets and exercises like the ones found in this book. When we help organizational clients with strategic planning or culture change, we often start by helping them reflect on the current state of their business. When we work with individuals, we do the same, often by using a tool called the Wheel of Life. Not to be confused with the concept of the Wheel of Life from Tibetan Buddhism, the Wheel of Life was created by Paul J. Meyer, father of self-improvement and entrepreneur. The idea is to reflect on the current state of your life based on several categories and score each one based on how you feel about each category today and how you want to feel about each category in the future. For example:

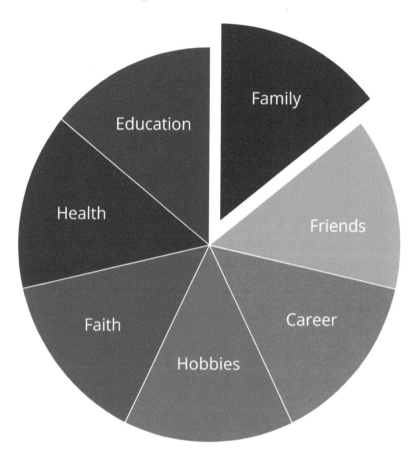

I'm currently feeling 9 out of 10 about my family but 3 out of 10 about friends. In the future, I'd like to still feel about a 9 about my family, but I want to feel about a 5 in the friends category. Based on these scores, I may want to invest more time and energy into my friendships.

By reflecting on the current state of your life and where you want to focus in the future, it gives you a visual way to describe where you want to invest your money, time, and energy. You may use it to see if your wheel is balanced or if it is out of balance with where you want to be.

To review your thoughts, actions, and impact, find a technique that works for you. Be pragmatic. If having a pretty journal filled with inspirational quotes is your thing, do it. If you'd rather start a blog, do so. If you'd rather talk to other people and take a few notes, great. My wife is a graphic recorder and facilitator, so she draws pictures as a way of reflecting on her thoughts, actions, and impact. Long story short, be ruthlessly pragmatic: do what works for you.

LEARNING FROM EXPERIENCE

Once we reflect on our experience, we have a chance to learn from it and maybe change our behavior in the future. Here's the thing: our behaviors, our thoughts, and our emotions have a physical component, including the neurons, or the wiring, in our brains. We are wired to think, feel, and act a certain way. That means to change our behavior, we must create new wiring and new connections. Deciding is not enough. Action and repetition, over time, are required for us to learn. Want to be a better listener? It means listening a lot. Over and over again, until you create enough wiring in your brain to do so automatically.

Learning is not just a mental skill; it is a physical skill as well. We have to create new connections to act on what we've learned.

Let's say you are trying to change your behavior from getting angry and snapping at others to pausing and listening.

1. First requirement: Notice your behaviors.
2. Second requirement: Understand your triggers; know which of your buttons are getting pushed.
3. Third requirement: Choose a different response, repeatedly, until you've developed a new way of responding.

Learning requires time, energy, and most of all, practice. This is why most people struggle to exercise, quit smoking, or eat differently. It's tough, and your brain doesn't want to change.

Learning from experience draws lessons from the review of our thoughts, actions, and impact. In some ways, it's like watching a video of our performance like actors and athletes do, observing what went right, what went wrong, and what we want to do differently next time. Watch the tape and decide what you want to work on or do differently in the future. For example, let's say you review your thoughts, actions, and impact and realize you don't listen well and don't understand what other people think, feel, or need. You see that you do this in a variety of settings, at work and at home. You decide it is a skill you want to master because you want other people to feel as if you care about them. Learning from experience would be reviewing the video and identifying the factors that led you to listen or not listen, to make judgments about when you were effective and when you could have been more effective, and identifying your own barriers to listening.

REFLECTING BEYOND TODAY

Practicing Reflection can extend beyond one day. You can reflect back on a month, a year, or your entire life. We all have identities formed through experience and how others perceive us. Understanding how experiences have shaped us can help us build a clearer picture of who we are and who we could be.

For example, consider your values as well as the beliefs and assumptions they are built on. What significant events in your life shaped those values, beliefs, and assumptions? For each event, how did it shape who you are and what you believe?

Sometimes it helps to sketch out a timeline of significant events and to describe the impact of those events. For example:

The first benefit of a timeline like this is that it can help us describe the themes that have shaped us over time and raise our awareness of what we really believe. One of the events that had a significant impact on my life was my first job, at 10 years old, working for my grandfather. He owned a repair shop, and each morning I would catch a ride at 6:00 a.m. with one of the mechanics. I'd work about 10 hours each day, sweeping up, helping the mechanics, steam-cleaning parts, and helping my grandmother fix lunch for all the employees. At the time, we didn't have much, and I made a dollar an hour, or 50 dollars a week. For a 10-year-old who never had money, it was a fortune. By the end of the summer, I had a better TV than my parents did. Although I can't imagine my kids working 50 hours a week as 10-year-olds, the experience reinforced my values of responsibility, hard work, and independence. Those values have made me successful, and as I've mentioned before, they also have a dark side.

The second benefit of Practicing Reflection using a timeline is that while the events in our lives may have shaped us, they do not define us. There is an idea in adult learning and psychology that we are self-authors. We write our own storylines, complete with heroes and villains, and we determine what impact those events have on us. It's a pretty advanced way of thinking about our lives, especially the idea that we can choose what story we tell and determine how events have impacted us. As Dr. Reina says, "We have a lot of BS narratives in our head that we have to manage."

As an example, consider the key events that strongly influenced who you are. Now imagine what other stories you could tell about those events. Could you have experienced the same events and come to a different conclusion? Going back to the example of working 10 hours a day as a 10-year-old, one way to interpret these events would be to pity me. To say that I should have been playing or focused on being a kid. That working a 50-hour week isn't great for adults and certainly not for kids—we have labor laws for a reason.

I don't think of it that way. I think that job strengthened me, not weakened me. That it taught me to take care of myself, to be responsible, and that I had control over my destiny. Even buying a television was incredibly empowering for a kid. The downsides are that I don't ask for help, I struggle to rely on others, and I have a hard time believing anyone will take care of me. I have what you might describe as an overdeveloped sense of responsibility, which is a heavy load to carry sometimes.

In the future, as I evolve, I may make other meanings from those same experiences. I may begin to tell an entirely different story based on the same events—that is, I will be the author of my own tale and will decide how I interpret my own life. It goes back to choice: we can decide what kind of person we are and act on that decision in the moment and over time.

APPLY THE LESSONS

Applying the lessons we draw from our experience is about practice. Remember, it takes time and repetition to form new connections and new habits. We will likely be clunky and awkward when we try something new. For example, if we are learning how to listen more effectively, it will likely feel awkward to slow down and understand what someone else is trying to communicate. It might feel inefficient or like a waste of time. It will be strange. We might fail again and again. Eventually, we will master the skill, like building a muscle. In martial arts, you quickly learn to fight;

however, mastering something as simple as a punch can take years as you slowly perfect the skill and build the muscle memory to do so. The same is true for any sport and many leadership skills.

When we practice new skills, we go through an awkward phase, then a mechanical phase, and finally an instinctive phase. When it's awkward and mechanical, we must consciously remember and choose to act on the skill. It's in this first awkward phase that most people quit because it's difficult and we feel like a phony. When leaders are practicing new skills, be it listening or giving feedback or describing their vision or using empathy, they will often worry about seeming inauthentic. "It's not me," they say, which is also a convenient excuse for not changing, not learning, and not growing. That's why it's skilled authenticity—you can be authentic and ineffective, or you can be both skilled and authentic. To do so takes practice and resilience during those awkward and mechanical phases.

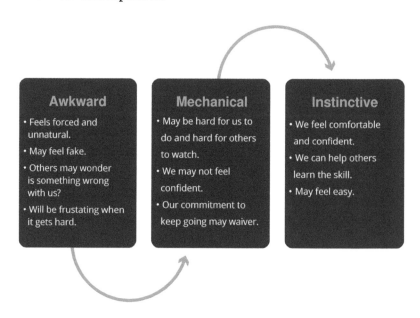

Awkward
- Feels forced and unnatural.
- May feel fake.
- Others may wonder is something wrong with us?
- Will be frustating when it gets hard.

Mechanical
- May be hard for us to do and hard for others to watch.
- We may not feel confident.
- Our commitment to keep going may waiver.

Instinctive
- We feel comfortable and confident.
- We can help others learn the skill.
- May feel easy.

One thing to keep in mind about applying the lessons. We are all messy works in progress. We are all imperfect, slowly growing and learning all the time. Hopefully, we get it right more than we get it wrong, but we will fail; we all do. Assume it will be difficult. Making any kind of deep and fundamental change in our lives takes work, effort, and most of all, choice. Situations can change us, circumstances can drive us, and relationships can move us; we can be the leaders for ourselves that we hope for and look for in others. We can be our own cheerleader, our own coach, our own visionary. We are the driver, we are the captain, we are the general; we are the author of our story and we are the guide in our own lives. Why wait when *we* are exactly what *we* need?

KEY TAKEAWAYS

Practicing Reflection includes three behaviors:

1. Reviewing your thoughts, actions, and impact
2. Learning from experience
3. Applying the lessons

Practicing Reflection helps us learn from our previous experiences, draw inspiration and lessons from our successes and our failures, and apply that learning to our future choices.

CHAPTER 9

Putting It All Together

Why does using all Five Practices of Values Based Leadership matter?

The practices are interdependent; when used together, they multiply your effectiveness.

BUILD AWARENESS

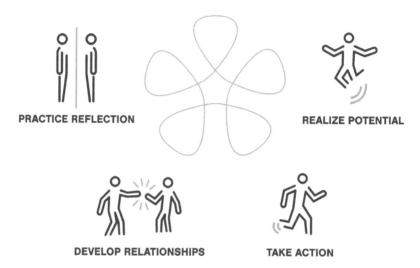

PRACTICE REFLECTION

REALIZE POTENTIAL

DEVELOP RELATIONSHIPS

TAKE ACTION

The Five Practices of Values Based Leadership are:

1. Building Awareness
2. Realizing Potential
3. Developing Relationships
4. Taking Action
5. Practicing Reflection

These practices are interdependent—they naturally complement and strengthen one another when used together. Building Awareness helps us develop relationships, just as Realizing Potential helps inform Taking Action. The Five Practices of Values Based Leadership are not linear; they occur simultaneously in no particular order. The best way to start is to start.

In order to illustrate how these practices work together, the following is a story pulled from some of our experiences working with clients over the years on the use of Values Based Leadership.

FIVE PRACTICES IN ACTION

William was the director of sales, and like many people in his position he was direct, fast-moving, and did not get bogged down in the details. Emma was the production manager; she was detail-oriented, structured, and preferred being right to going fast. For William, customers came first, no matter their demands, and he believed it was the organization's job to serve them and serve them well. For Emma, customers mattered, but so did processes and fairness. When William went around her to ask her people to rush a customer's order, their simmering feud came to a head.

During their last leadership team meeting, she asked him to stay a few extra minutes.

"What are you doing?" Emma demanded. "That order forced us to rush one customer to the front of the line. We had to bend over backward to take care of them. In the meantime, other customers had to wait on their products to make your customer happy."

"Customers come first," William said. "If this customer needs their product quickly, we need to do it. Otherwise, he will go somewhere else."

"What about all of our other customers? Don't they matter?" Emma said.

"Sure, but they will understand," said William.

"Why would they understand?" asked Emma. "I don't understand, and I work here. It's not fair to other customers, and it's not fair to my team."

"That customer needed us. We delivered. I don't see the problem."

"That's because you never think of anyone but yourself and your customers," Emma snapped. "Why did you go around me?" she asked.

"You weren't around. This was a rush order, and the customer was in a hurry. It seemed fastest to go straight to your team."

"That's not the process."

"I don't see why it matters."

In that moment, Emma was angry and William was frustrated. They had stumbled into a core values conflict.

For William, it seemed simple. He valued service, speed, and flexibility. He also valued solving problems. In this instance, he could act on all of his values and feel great about doing so.

For Emma, William had betrayed everything she believed mattered. She valued processes and fairness. When William went around her and pushed his customer ahead of everyone else, he not only stepped on her toes but triggered all of her values hot buttons.

Objectively, it is right to serve customers, to be flexible and meet their needs quickly. It is also right to follow processes and to administer them fairly. In this case, William and Emma could have handled the conflict more effectively, but their conflict would remain the same.

In the real story, William and Emma's conflict continued to escalate, although eventually they smoothed things over. It's the kind of values conflict that plays out every day in our workplaces, families, and communities. If William and Emma were given a do-over, how could they have resolved this conflict using the Five Practices?

To resolve this conflict, William and Emma could start with Building Awareness by recognizing what they each valued in this situation and how it drove their behaviors.

Second, they could remember the impact they want to have on others. They each want to be an effective leader. They realize how important the other person is in how they serve customers. Neither one wants to carry a grudge against the other, even if they have different core values.

Third, they could each focus on Developing Relationships by understanding what is important to the other person in this situation and empathizing with them. They could also consider how to make the other person successful in this situation by helping them feel heard and resolving their needs.

Fourth, they need to face this challenge and not ignore it. A conflict like this will not simply go away. It will come up again and again because William and Emma value different things. Also, they still need to be clear about what is important to them and act on their values but with the other person in mind.

Finally, they need to begin Practicing Reflection and apply the lessons they learn in this situation not just to their relationship but to future interactions with other people.

More simply, even though he valued service, speed, and flexibility, William did not have to rush his customer to the front of the line. Even if he did so, he did not have to go around Emma and straight to her team. He could have communicated his need to her, and they could have found a way to resolve the issue. He could have been more aware in the moment and made more conscious choices about how he led through the issue.

Emma could have also been more aware. On hearing about William's actions, Emma could have considered William's values and empathized with his need to serve their customers. She could have been curious and asked him a few questions to better understand why he did what he did. She still needed to stand up for herself and her team's processes, however, but she could have done so in a courageous but respectful manner that would make it more likely that William would come to her in the future.

Change always starts with us.

DEVELOPING YOUR OWN PRACTICES

Whenever someone wants to begin their own Values Based Leadership journey, I often recommend a combination of workshops, instruments, and coaching. Yet, these practices require no outside resources to use them; you can follow this book and build your own ways to follow the practices. However, there are some tools that can help you on your journey.

Building Awareness is complemented by tools such as personality assessments, core values exercises, and 360 feedback instruments. A great way to start is by sharing your goals with people you trust who also see you in action. Then ask for their advice and feedback about how you can achieve those goals. They can be long-term goals over the course of your career or they can be short-term, in-the-moment goals, such as how you want to show up for a meeting. When people share their advice and feedback with you, take notes. Your instinct may be to deny, defend, deflect, or explain why you do what you do, but it's unhelpful and discourages feedback in the future. When they are finished, say thank you because they have given you the gift of data you can use to improve your performance and achieve your goals.

WHAT ARE YOUR GOALS, IN THE MOMENT OR OVER TIME?	WHAT ADVICE AND FEEDBACK HAVE YOU RECEIVED THAT CAN HELP YOU REACH THOSE GOALS?

Realizing Potential can be supplemented by purpose and vision exercises and enacted through individual development plans. Realizing Potential is activated by Practicing Reflection. Look back over your life for themes: what has consistently inspired you? What are you good at doing and excited to do? Then look ahead: what excites you about the future? What impact do you want to have on others? As you look ahead, also describe the best version of yourself and your leadership.

WHAT IS YOUR PURPOSE?	WHAT IMPACT DO YOU WANT TO HAVE ON OTHERS?	DESCRIBE THE BEST VERSION OF YOURSELF.

Developing Relationships can be aided by reading the personality assessments of others, doing your own listening assessments, and observing the impact your actions have on others and asking for their feedback. A best practice for Developing Relationships starts with identifying the relationships you want to work on, whether personal or professional. Ideally, you would establish a shared vision with the other person about what kind of relationship you want to have. It may sound corny, but this conversation allows you to establish boundaries and expectations that you can both work toward. If it is not safe to do it this way, at a minimum determine what kind of relationship you want to have with the other person and work toward it.

Next, consider the person's style and values. How might you adapt your behavior to be more effective in communicating and relating to them? How might you be curious and get to know them better so you can empathize and understand how they feel and why they feel the way they do? Finally, put your thinking into action and observe the impact your behaviors have on the relationship over time. Remember, you can influence other people, but you can't control them, and don't solely use their reaction to evaluate your own efforts.

WHO DO YOU WANT TO STRENGTHEN YOUR RELATIONSHIP WITH?	WHAT IS YOUR VISION FOR THE RELATIONSHIP?	WHAT IS THIS PERSON'S STYLE? WHAT DO THEY VALUE?	HOW WILL YOU ADAPT YOUR APPROACH TO BE MORE EFFECTIVE WITH THIS PERSON?

Taking Action is about making conscious choices that align with your values despite challenges or setbacks. Part of Taking Action is Practicing Reflection: are you making choices that align with your values? Are there challenges you are not facing but instead avoiding? To catalyze your own actions, build a relationship with someone who will be your accountability partner, who can call you out on your stuff, especially if you make excuses for not acting on your values or not dealing with conflict. That person can be a professional, like a coach, or informal, like a peer or friend. Remember, courage doesn't mean you aren't afraid. Courage means taking action despite your fears.

WHAT CHALLENGE DO I NEED TO FACE?	WHICH OF MY VALUES ARE INVOLVED?	WHAT CAN I DO TO FACE THIS CHALLENGE BY ACTING ON MY VALUES?	WHO CAN I ASK TO HELP ME BE ACCOUNTABLE FOR FACING THIS CHALLENGE?

Practicing Reflection is the art of pausing to look back, learning the lessons the past can teach us, and applying those lessons to the future. This can be activated through quiet meditation or boisterous conversations. A variety of tools can help you reflect, including worksheets, exercises, and this book. Consider what you have done, how you felt, and what impact you made. Did you achieve what you wanted to achieve? What did your experience teach you? What will you do next time you have an opportunity?

REFLECT ON YOUR THOUGHTS, ACTIONS, AND IMPACT.	WHAT DID YOU LEARN FROM YOUR EXPERIENCE?	WHAT WILL YOU DO NEXT TIME?

When it comes to your leadership journey, the most important thing is finding what works for you. There is no one right answer, but there are many right paths. You may have to experiment, try various approaches, and see what works. It's your development, after all, and it stands to reason that you should find what works for you.

This journey is a powerful one; it has transformed my life for the better and helped me become the kind of person my wife, kids, and I can be proud of. My hope is that you too start such a journey, and I promise you, it will be worth the effort. Whether you are a formal leader in an organization or just someone who wants to be a better person, our growth starts with a choice to work on ourselves first and to take responsibility for our choices and the impact we have on others. It's one of the most important choices we will ever make.

Leadership is a choice, not a title.
And leadership starts when we
choose to work on ourselves.

A STORY ABOUT VALUES BASED LEADERSHIP

It's Sunday morning, and I'm in the kitchen feeding my six-week-old baby, Xander. I'm holding him awkwardly because everything you do as a brand-new dad is awkward. I'm desperately trying to find my sea legs—my parenting sea legs—and I'm up early so my wife can sleep while I do my job as a dad. He's struggling with the bottle and I'm struggling giving it to him when my wife comes down the stairs. She's bleary-eyed, hair akimbo, looking like she'd rather be back in bed for just a few minutes more. She stops on the next-to-last step, takes one look at me and the mess I am making of feeding time and shouts, "Don't do it that way!"

My wife and I have big personalities and strong opinions. Usually, when one of us snipes at the other, we get louder and louder, convinced the other person hasn't heard us because they don't agree. By shouting at me, she was inviting me to a fight. But this time, I was holding my son. And I had been steadily working on myself and my leadership. Not at home but at work. I'd been getting feedback on how closed-minded I could be, on how being right was the only thing that was important, and how emotionally closed I was to other people. Vulnerability and transparency were new tools in my toolbox, and I looked like a toddler learning to ride a bike whenever I used them—sure it was cute, but everyone was convinced it was going to end in tears.

That Sunday morning, I had a moment of clarity—it did not have to be like this. I did not have to respond the way I always responded, by trying to be right in a loud voice. I did not want to ruin my relationship with my wife or with my son. If I wanted the path of our lives to be different, I had to be different. And so, I looked at my wife and made a conscious choice. It was probably one of the hardest things I've ever had to do, although it sounds simple now.

I looked at my wife, who was glaring at me from the steps. "Honey," I said, "all I want to be is a good husband and good father. Being good at this is really important to me. And when you yell at me, it makes me feel stupid. And when I feel stupid, I get angry, and when I get angry, I fight. And I don't want to fight."

My wife is a strong, capable, and confident woman.

She burst into tears. Through her tears she said, "You're a good husband and father, but I haven't slept in six weeks and I haven't had a shower and I'm so tired."

In that moment, our relationship changed. We were stuck in a dynamic that would not have ended well, for our marriage or for our kids. In that moment, we took a different path. That path started with a moment of awareness, a larger sense of potential, some understanding of relationships, and a bit of reflection, but mostly it started with a choice.

—DR. THOMAS EPPERSON, PRESIDENT, INNERWILL LEADERSHIP INSTITUTE

Epilogue

Imagine yourself once more—confident in the path you are on, open to the bends and curves ahead. Working each day to be a little bit better, under no illusion that you are perfect but not paralyzed by anxiety that you have to be. Comfortable in your own skin and willing to grow.

Imagine others once more, extraordinary not because they are superhuman but because they are not. Filled with the potential to be amazing.

Once again, imagine a workplace where people are happy and engaged. Where they feel valued and committed to the organization's goals. Where they have the skills they need to do their jobs. Where they enjoy the work they do and the people they do it with.

Now imagine a world where everyone takes a moment to think about the impact they could have and then act on it. Where everyone makes a few more choices to help, to inspire, to connect. To lead others in creating stronger families, communities, and institutions. Who choose to work first on themselves and then to help others. Who stand up for what they value and when they get knocked down—and they will—who get back up. Who have found the just-right place between the courage to act and compassion for others.

You can lead. Not because you are more talented, smarter, or more creative than the rest of us, but because you choose to do so. You choose to have a few more better days than bad, to work on yourself, and to have a positive impact on others. You choose to act on what you value, even when the world is telling you to sit down, to be quiet, or to wait your turn. This book is about developing your inner will to be and do amazing things. Things we desperately need in our workplaces, families, and communities.

We hope you will choose to follow the practices of Values Based Leadership. We hope you will develop your inner will to be and do amazing things.

It all starts with a choice.

Additional Tools

PERSONAL TIMELINE

1. Identify five key events in your life; those significant things that helped to shape you.

2. Note the year and a few words that describe the event.

3. Consider the influence these events had in shaping you; how might they connect to who you are today?

DISCOVER YOUR CORE VALUES

Core values are deeply personal and require observation and reflection to identify and understand. They are formed when we are children and develop as we grow and learn. This exercise helps to examine the values that drive our behaviors.

YOUR VALUES IN ACTION

1. Review and consider the importance of each value.

2. Circle the values that are important to you and cross out those that are not.

3. If you can't find one of your values, write it in the space provided at the end of the list.

4. Write your top five core values below.

TOP 5 CORE VALUES

1. _____

2. _____

3. _____

4. _____

5. _____

VALUES

Accomplishment	Decisiveness	Hope	Relaxation
Accountability	Effectiveness	Independence	Reputation
Accuracy	Efficiency	Individuality	Resourcefulness
Achievement	Environment	Influencing Others	Respect
Activeness	Excellence	Integrity	Responsibility
Advancement	Excitement	Intelligence	Results
Adventure	Fairness	Involvement	Safety
Aesthetics	Fame	Joy	Security
Affection	Family	Justice	Self-respect
Appreciation	Financial Security	Knowledge	Service
Authenticity	Free Time	Leadership	Significance
Authority	Free Will	Learning	Sophistication
Balance	Freedom	Love	Spirituality
Challenge	Friendships	Loyalty	Stability
Clarity	Fun	Meaningful Work	Status
Collaboration	Generosity	Modesty	Tradition
Community	Grace	Optimism	Variety
Compassion	Growth	Order	Wealth
Competence	Hard Work	Patriotism	Wisdom
Competition	Harmony	Positivity	Well-being
Control	Health	Power	Relaxation
Courage	Helping Others	Privacy	
Creativity	Honesty	Quality of Work	
Curiosity	Honor	Relationships	

PUT YOUR VALUES TO WORK

InnerWill believes leadership is a choice, not a title, a conscious choice that begins with building our awareness of self. Braver leaders consistently make this choice to better understand themselves—to ensure they live, work, and lead in alignment with their core values, and to ignite the potential in themselves and others. This exercise helps to examine the values that drive our behaviors.

YOUR VALUES IN ACTION

1. Rewrite the top five core values you identified in the Discover exercise.

2. On your own or with others, consider the questions shown.

TOP 5 CORE VALUES

1. _____

2. _____

3. _____

4. _____

5. _____

Q. What are examples of behaviors that demonstrate your values in action?

A.

Q. How do your current behaviors not reflect your values?

A.

Q. What is one thing you can do today that demonstrates at least one of your values?

A.

Name _____

Date _____

Practicing Feedback Skills

Connect with at least three people, and ask them for three words that describe you at your best and three that describe you at your worst.

FEEDBACK PROVIDER	YOU AT YOUR BEST	YOU AT YOUR WORST
	1. 2. 3.	1. 2. 3.
	1. 2. 3.	1. 2. 3.

REFLECTION

Were there any surprises? Any themes?

What questions do you have receiving the above feedback?

Acknowledgments

This book would not be possible without the team at InnerWill, including Sharon Amoss, Wendy Berenson, Carla Ruiz, Kim Jones, Britten Parker, Wanda Ortwine, and Betsey Fortlouis. The stories, quotes, and examples come from a wide range of board members, clients, supporters, mentors, and friends, all of whom have helped me in too many ways to recount here. This book, like our leadership institute, has its roots in Luck Companies, a 100-year-old family business that puts everything in the preceding pages into action every day. With nearly two decades of work by our associates on themselves and on their leadership in the business and at home, we can confidently say that Values Based Leadership works. Most importantly, I could not do what I do every day without the love and support of my wife and our two sons.

About the Author

DR. THOMAS EPPERSON is the president of InnerWill Leadership Institute and has over 20 years of experience as a leadership coach, facilitator, and speaker, and he regularly works with clients to help transform leaders and their organizations.

Tom is a certified business coach and has a doctorate in leadership from The George Washington University. Tom is currently an instructor in Virginia Commonwealth University's Executive MBA Program.

Tom believes that leadership is a choice, not a title, and that our responsibility as leaders is to make a positive difference in the lives of those around us. Tom balances high expectations of himself and others with relentless optimism about the ability of individuals to make our organizations, families, and communities amazing places to live, work, and grow. Tom believes that leadership is a powerful force for good in the world, if we choose to do so; his personal mission in life is to help others develop the skills to make that choice more often than not.

Tom works hard to be a great husband and father; he's married to a strong, creative woman and has two fantastic sons who have taught him that we can learn as much about ourselves and our leadership at home as we can at work.

About InnerWill
Leadership Institute

Born out of Luck Companies, InnerWill Leadership Institute was founded to teach other leaders how to build values-based organizations that ignite the potential in people. After an 85-year history as a successful business, President and CEO Charlie Luck, IV realized that the business had so much more potential if the alignment and collaboration of senior management could be improved. This led to a Values Based Leadership (VBL) journey—for his family and for the workplace. Ultimately, the VBL principles and practices were shared with every employee at Luck Companies and every Luck family member. As a result, Luck Companies is the oldest and largest family-held and family-run aggregate business in the country, ranks in the top three most engaged places to work in the United States, and is a thriving organization built for the future.

The impact to Luck Companies, and to the individuals touched and transformed by the VBL journey, inspired the launch of InnerWill. Today, InnerWill teaches the necessary skills to strengthen leadership capabilities and drive results through the practice of VBL. More than a training company, InnerWill is a 501(c)(3) nonprofit that invests in the organizations and people it serves through personalized solutions built to ensure positive and measurable impacts.

VBL motivates and inspires employees by connecting organizational goals to employees' core values. Companies that foster a values-based approach to leadership create connections that have a significant impact on organizational outcomes, including higher levels of engagement, lower levels of turnover, increased alignment around a company's strategy and mission, and a better bottom line. Using VBL as a foundation, InnerWill helps develop leaders' abilities to overcome challenges, leverage opportunities, and achieve goals. Our programs are designed and tested to be accessible and practical and to achieve transformative change. Sustainable change rarely comes from helping just one person; that's why our facilitators are trained to go deep into companies, from the boardroom to the factory floor, across roles and across generations to multiply impact. InnerWill has worked with more than 350 organizations and the families behind them to overcome business challenges and drive success through VBL.

LEADERSHIP INSTITUTE

InnerWill is a 501c3 leadership institute that has helped hundreds of organizations and the thousands of people who work there, actualize potential, maximize performance and elevate impact. We believe leadership is a choice, not a title. That's why we work hard to develop better people, braver leaders, and a wiser world through Values Based Leadership. This transformational process enables people to work, lead and live in alignment with their core values, while helping others to do the same. Our programs and services help organizations generate stronger reputations and better bottom lines. InnerWill was born out of Luck Companies, the nation's largest family-held and family-run aggregate business and one of the top three most engaged places to work in the US.

BETTER PERSON, BRAVER LEADER, WISER WORLD

InnerWill Leadership Institute

P.O. BOX 334, Manakin-Sabot, VA 23103

844.898.WILL

www.innerwill.org

CPSIA information can be obtained
at www.ICGtesting.com
Printed in the USA
BVHW090214100522
635695BV00002B/12/J

9 781544 526812